MW01489299

Fondue Cookbook
for Beginners

Turn Your Ordinary Dinners into Tasty Evenings.
Over 120 Simple and Creative Fondue Recipes to Delight
You and Your Loved Ones

By

Sophia Boutren

Table of Contents

Introduction

Among the endless opportunities to explore different cultures' flavors and traditions, there is something special about that particular dish called fondue. It transcends generations and brings people together for a shared feast of delicious melted foods, offering a unique and memorable culinary experience encompassing food and human connection in one context.

Through this book, you will take a journey into the fascinating world of fondue, exploring its variations and learning how to create delicious and memorable events that engage the taste senses and foster lasting memories.

Our inspiration stems from a deep passion for the communal table and a desire to help others experience their moments of culinary delight. Whether you are a beginner in the kitchen or an experienced cook, the entire book is designed to guide you in making your fondue from scratch with a collection of delicious and easy-to-follow recipes.

First, we'll explain the history and origins of fondue, recommend the best sauces and side dishes to serve with it, and warn you about common mistakes to avoid. We'll also delve into the various types of equipment needed for fondue preparation and explain step-by-step how to throw a successful fondue dinner.

Concluding this general part, you will find several mouth-watering fondue recipes, from the classic cheese to chocolate fondue for dessert lovers, from savory oil-based fondues to delicious broth-based fondues.

Each recipe will take you to a different corner of the world, allowing you to enjoy countless new flavors right from your table. It also has detailed instructions for each recipe, so you can confidently create a perfect fondue for any occasion.

As you become passionate about fondue, you will discover the pleasure of creating exceptional dishes and the excitement of sharing them with your friends and loved ones, forging ever closer bonds.

From family gatherings to dinners with friends, from romantic dinners to lively parties, fondues can bring people together, resulting in engaging conversations and fun evenings; they are, in fact, versatile, accommodating, and, above all, delicious.

The book aims to allow the reader to customize his fondue recipes, using ingredients according to his tastes and preferences.

He will embark on an incredible culinary adventure and discover one of the most wonderful ways to spend time with the people he loves most. So, let the journey begin, and may fondue ignite your craving for good food and sharing.

Welcome to the world of fondue, where every dip is a step toward creating unforgettable moments.

Chapter 1: What is fondue and how to prepare it

1.1 The origins of Fondue

Fondue, a culinary sensation that has warmed hearts and ignited palates for centuries, is much more than a dish. It's an experience that fosters connections, encourages interaction, and celebrates the joy of communal dining.

This iconic Swiss creation has a history that dates back to the early days of alpine life, and its evolution into a global sensation is a testament to its enduring appeal. At its essence, fondue is a method of sharing and enjoying various foods by dipping them into a pot of melted goodness.

The term "fondue" is derived from the French word "fondre," meaning "to melt," and its origins are deeply intertwined with the rustic and hearty lifestyles of the Swiss and French Alpine regions.

Communal dining practices were born out of necessity in these mountainous terrains, where harsh winters and limited resources prevailed. The earliest forms of fondue were practical solutions to use stale bread and aged cheeses, which were melted to create a nourishing and hearty meal. The method of communal dipping allowed for shared sustenance, especially during the cold months when food resources were scarce.

The classic Swiss fondue features melted Gruyère and Emmental cheeses, white wine, and a touch of Kirsch for flavor. The mixture is dissolved in a communal pot over an open flame and served alongside cubes of bread for dipping.

This traditional cheese fondue quickly gained popularity and became a symbol of friendliness and warmth, ideally suited for gatherings of friends and family.

Beyond Switzerland, fondue gained international recognition during the mid-20th century, becoming an emblematic dish associated with conviviality, sharing, and indulgence. Savory fondues involving meats, vegetables, and broths emerged, each offering a unique twist on the communal dining experience.

Additionally, sweet renditions using melted chocolate for dipping fruits, and other delectable treats captured the hearts of dessert enthusiasts everywhere.

1.2 The different kinds of fondue

We examine the different types of savory fondues in this paragraph.

Cheese fondue

With their distinct flavors and textures, cheeses come together in a smooth explosion of flavors. A subtle whisper of white wine infuses the blend, elevating the richness and depth of the dining experience.

The pot sits over a gentle flame, emitting a warm, inviting glow as the cheese transforms into a velvety river of goodness. You grab a skewer and skewer a cube of rustic bread, anxiously awaiting the moment of dipping. The moment bread meets cheese, time seems to stop; the cheese wraps the bread and coats it in a way tantalizes your senses.

The friendly nature of cheese fondue creates an atmosphere of shared enjoyment as friends and family gather to dip and savor every bite.

Oil fondue

Imagine a table with colorful vegetables, succulent meats, and a pot of glistening golden oil. A tantalizing aroma envelops your senses while the meat sizzles and cooks right before your eyes. Dipping and cooking become an enthralling ritual as each morsel of meat is transformed into a crunchy, flavorful delight.

Accompanying sauces allow you to personalize each bite with bursts of vibrant flavor. It is a unique experience as you become the chef of your culinary adventure.

Broth fondue

Now, move over to a boiling cauldron of fragrant broth on a table surrounded by your friends. Thin slices of tender chicken or beef and seafood are ready to be immersed in the broth. Each sauce transforms meats into succulent, melt-in-your-mouth morsels. The variety of accompanying sauces allows you to experiment with new tastes and flavors.

Types of sweet fondue

Now, let's look at the different types of sweet fondue.

Chocolate fondue is a concoction of dark and milk chocolate, creating a velvety pool of indulgence that invites you to dig in without hesitation; next to it, you can put a series of bananas, strawberries, marshmallows, and pieces of cake waiting to be enveloped by the warm liquid of chocolate and milk.

Caramel fondue gives a particular buttery aroma that gives the sauce a velvety richness, which crisp apple slices, slices of cake, and pretzels can accompany. With each taste, you will discover a delicious contrast between the silkiness and the crunchiness of the foods you accompany it with.

Fruit fondue can be made of ripe strawberries, pieces of pineapple, and orange segments; every bite is an explosion of natural sweetness and freshness.

1.3 The main techniques of fondue preparation

The foundation for creating a successful fondue lies in sourcing quality ingredients and using the necessary tools.

A deep heat-resistant fondue pot or an electric fondue set is indispensable for oil fondue. Additionally, you should use high-quality cooking oil, such as vegetable, peanut, or canola oil, to achieve your desired cooking temperature without compromising the flavors. You should also select different types of proteins and vegetables that go with the chosen fondue theme.

It is necessary to create an environment that favors communal meals and follow a series of guidelines, such as:

- place the fondue pot in the center of the table, ensuring that it is easily accessible to all participants;
- provide large forks or fondue skewers for dipping and plates and napkins for each guest;
- accurately place condiments, sauces and accompaniments;
- make sure the fondue pot is placed on a stable, heat-resistant surface;
- handle the pan and forks carefully, using the appropriate holders to avoid burns. If you are using electric fondue sets, follow the manufacturer's instructions;
- Ensure a well-ventilated space to create a safe cooking environment.
- reach the ideal oil temperature. In this regard, use a kitchen thermometer and heat the oil to the recommended temperature based on the chosen recipe.
- provide a variety of complementary dipping sauces to enhance the flavors and increase the pleasantness of the experience. Remember, finally, it is essential to balance the ingredients, providing a careful selection of proteins, vegetables, and fruit.

1.4 How important is wine?

Do you want to know a secret ingredient that is more than just an accompaniment but is an essential element for creating a perfect fondue? With its rich history and diverse flavors, wine is fundamental to preparing fondue.

If you add a splash of wine to cheese fondue, the alcohol gently evaporates and leaves light layers of flavor that enrich the taste of the cheese. In practice, the acidity of wine creates a perfect balance of textures and flavors; a blend of ingredients goes beyond the culinary aspect.

The wine takes a backseat in the oil fondue, allowing the spotlight to shine on the sizzling meat and accompanying sauces. In any case, a good wine on the table adds a touch of elegance and refinement, raising the overall level of the meal.

For broth fondue, the wine again makes the difference, as it goes well with the flavorful character of the broth.

In the world of fondue, wine becomes a catalyst that enhances the flavors and transports you to the heart of ancient European culinary traditions.

1.5 The elements needed to prepare fondue

In this section we will look at the ingredients, sauces and gravies needed to make savory and sweet fondue.

1.5.1 The ingredients for preparing savory fondue

The heart of every savory fondue lies in the ingredients immersed in hot oil or broth.

Select a variety of proteins, vegetables, and breads that harmonize with your chosen dining theme. You may consider thinly sliced chicken, beef, shrimp, or tofu for protein.

You can consider peppers, broccoli, asparagus, and mushrooms for vegetables.

As for the bread, it uses crunchy artisan bread cubes.

Sauces and gravies elevate the flavor profile of fondue, adding complexity and depth of flavor. Here is a range of options to suit different preferences.

1) Teriyaki sauce.

A sweet and savory sauce that adds a touch of umami, ideal for Asian-inspired fondue.

2) Garlic aioli.

A creamy garlic sauce that adds richness and spiciness to savory morsels.

3) Remoulade sauce.

A spicy and structured accompaniment, excellent for fish and vegetable fondue.

4) Spicy peanut sauce.

A bold, bold choice with a balance of heat and nuttiness, perfect for combining protein and veggies.

5) Herb and lemon sauce.

A light and refreshing choice which combines notes of citrus and fragrant herbs to give a Mediterranean touch to the dish.

1.5.2 The types of meat to use

Regarding fondue, you have many meat options to tantalize your taste buds. You can consider beef perfect for dipping into hot fondue, or if you prefer a leaner choice, chicken offers a very delicate alternative. Pork slices provide the most flavor, while venison adds a unique, gamey flavor.

1.5.3 The types of cheese to use

Choosing the right cheese is vital to a satisfying fondue. The Swiss cheese, with its sweet notes, is a timeless favorite. Gruyere, with its rich and complex flavor, is an excellent complement. Emmental, known for its creamy consistency, pairs well with various ingredients. Cheddar brings a spicy and bold element to the table for those looking for a bolder flavor.

1.5.4 Vegetables that can accompany the fondue

To balance the flavors and textures, a selection of vegetables pairs beautifully with the fondue. Broccoli, with its crunchy florets, adds a refreshing touch. With its delicate flavor, the cauliflower absorbs the essence of the fondue, the tender and earthy mushrooms go well with the cheese and broth sauces, and the peppers bring color and freshness to the entire dish. Finally, asparagus offers an elegant alternative for enthusiasts of this food.

1.6 The ingredients needed to prepare sweet fondue

The ingredients for sweet fondue revolve around delicious sauces that can be covered with delicious chocolate, fruit, or caramel-based sauces. You could consider a variety of options:

- fruit, such as strawberries, bananas, apple slices, and pieces of pineapple;

- slices of pound cake or brownie, which absorb chocolate or caramel sauce;
- soft marshmallows which take on a remarkable quality when dipped in hot chocolate or caramel.

Sauces and gravies for sweet fondue help to make the experience even more satisfying and tasty. You could offer several options, such as a chocolate sauce, a caramel sauce, or a mixed fruit arrangement. The chocolate and hazelnut spread will also guarantee a very delicious flavor.

The right choice of chocolate is necessary to indulge in a sweet fondue. Dark chocolate offers rich cocoa flavors that resonate with decadence. Milk chocolate, with its creamy sweetness, is ideal for dipping fruit and desserts. Flavored chocolates such as raspberry or salted caramel add an exciting twist to your dessert fondue.

1.7 The 10 most common mistakes to avoid when preparing fondue

1) Encouraging double dipping can lead to ingredient contamination and a less sanitary experience.

2) Using cheese with incorrect melting properties can result in a lumpy or separated fondue. Always choose cheeses known for their melting ability.

3) Not seasoning the fondue can result in a tasteless experience. Taste and adjust the seasoning, including salt and pepper, to ensure a consistently balanced flavor.

4) Do not prepare the bread, vegetables, and meat for dipping before beginning the fondue process.

5) Reheating cheese rapidly can ruin the texture and flavor. Slowly melt the cheese over medium-low heat to achieve a smooth consistency.

6) Don't add wine when preparing cheese fondue.

7) Not stirring the fondue frequently can make it stick to the bottom of the pot or cause an uneven mixture.

8) Using cold ingredients can cause fondue to become grainy or curdled. Allow ingredients such as cheese or wine to come to room temperature before combining.

9) Neglecting the consistency of the chocolate: When making chocolate fondue, not paying attention to the surface of the chocolate can lead to a thick or grainy sauce.

10) For meat fondue, failure to correctly adjust the temperature of the oil or broth can result in undercooked or overcooked meat.

Chapter 2: The tools needed for making fondue

2.1 The essential tools for making a fondue

Forks

The cornerstone of any fondue meal is the fondue fork. For guests to skewer and dip various foods into the melted mixtures, these tools are essential to the participatory aspect of fondue.

The long handle, which protects your hands from the heat of the fondue, is one of its distinctive qualities.

Fondue forks often include color-coded tips or handles for aesthetic and functional reasons. Color coding ensures visitors can quickly recognize their divisions to avoid ladle confusion. The resistant materials with which these forks are built guarantee simple and effective use.

Dishes

The purpose of fondue plates is to enhance the fondue experience by providing dipping products with a streamlined and easy way to dip. The segmented compartments of these dishes, each intended to accommodate a different type of dippable ingredient, give them their distinctive look.

The split prevents flavors from mixing and allows guests to enjoy each dip. Fondue plates make for a seamless and delicious dining experience while keeping the dipping process exciting and well-organized.

Heat resistant gloves

Heat-resistant gloves are essential when working with fondue pots with open flames or electric heating sources. These heat-resistant gloves are a barrier between your hands and hot components and can withstand extreme temperatures. The gloves make it safe for hosts or guests to handle the fondue pot without worrying about burns or pain.

Skimmers

Skimmers serve to remove any food debris that may accumulate in the fondue pot during the soaking process. By skimming the pool regularly, hosts can ensure that the fondue maintains its optimal consistency and remains free of debris that could alter its texture or flavor. They also contribute to the visual appeal of the fondue pot.

Bowls of sauce

Dip bowls serve as vessels for these delicious accompaniments, creating a convenient way to present different dipping options. Dip bowls allow guests to customize their dipping experience based on their preferences. Sauce bowls not only elevate the sensory aspects of fondue but also contribute to the aesthetic appeal of the entire setup.

Cheese fondue pot

These pans are specially made to help gradually melt cheese over medium-low heat. Their design features a large base and a smaller top to help distribute heat evenly and prevent the cheese from burning.

Many cheese fondue pots include a unique fondue burner, allowing guests to regulate the temperature and maintain the ideal consistency of the cheese throughout the dinner. Cookware made of durable and easy-to-clean materials, such as stainless steel, is preferable.

Meat fondue pot

Specialized pans are needed for anyone attempting to make meat fondue. These pots have high edges, which are necessary to contain the cooking oil for meat or broth. They also incorporate heat sources, such as burners or electric heating components, to maintain a consistent cooking temperature. The meat fondue pot must be usefully safe, ensuring that the oil or broth remains hot enough to cook the meat evenly and thoroughly.

Chocolate fondue pot

These pots are deeper than those used for cheese, as they must accommodate the melted chocolate and maintain the ideal dipping consistency.

Electric chocolate fondue pots have integrated heating components that offer perfect temperature control and ensure the smooth consistency of the chocolate. The features and design of the Chocolate Fondue Pot are designed to provide constant heating.

Electric fondue pot

The electric fondue pot is a flexible and practical choice for a contemporary version of traditional fondue. There is no need for an additional heat source because these pans include built-in heating components. The precise temperature control of electric fondue pots allows your fondue to maintain the optimal heat level throughout your meal. Electric pots are an affordable option, especially for those who want a quick fondue.

2.1.1 The characteristics and functions of fondue tools

The success of fondue tools, pots, and pans is based on several features.

The choice of material dramatically affects the functioning and durability of these tools. The advantages of stainless steel are longevity, equal heat distribution, and staining resistance. Enamel-coated options offer a smooth, hygienic surface, while cast iron is an excellent option for pans used over a flame for meat or cheese fondues, as it retains heat well.

Fondue pots that need an additional heat source often have a separate stovetop. These burners can work with gel or liquid alcohol and guarantee a constant heat source.

The size of the fondue pot is an essential factor and should be in line with the number of guests you wish to serve. In contrast, a smaller pot works better with a limited number of guests; a larger pot is undoubtedly more suitable for gatherings of many people.

The stability of pans is important because fondue is a social activity. Pots and pans with sturdy bases and handle that remain cool to the touch should be used to ensure safe handling.

2.2 Other useful fondue tools

A **fondue fountain** is one tool that turns the dessert fondue experience into a captivating spectacle. Its arrangement allows the melted chocolate to continuously flow downwards, producing a genuinely beautiful sight; fruit, marshmallows, and pieces of cake are the most common things people dip into fondue fountains.

The cascading action of the layers causes the melted chocolate to fall evenly and smoothly, motivating guests to participate in the dipping activity. They can interact directly with the chocolate fountain by choosing the treats to dip into the flowing chocolate. In addition, the fondue fountain forms a central element that attracts attention and gives the table a touch of refinement.

Another convenient tool is the **chocolate tempering machine**. It offers precise temperature control, enabling guests to set and maintain the optimal temperatures required for tempering. This ensures that the chocolate retains its shine and soft texture throughout the dipping process.

In essence, the machines guide the chocolate through distinct melting and cooling phases, ensuring the correct formation of the cocoa butter crystals. The result is a visually attractive chocolate with a well-solidified consistency.

2.3 Where to purchase fondue tools

Fondue tools can be purchased in a variety of ways. Below, you can find a detailed list.

1) Specialized kitchen utensil shops

These shops often contain a department dedicated only to fondue equipment, such as fondue fountains and chocolate tempering equipment. Seeing the equipment up close, knowing its features, and getting specialized support from trained employees are all benefits of going to such places.

2) Online retailers

An easy way to purchase fondue machines is through online e-commerce. You can make informed judgments from the comfort of your home thanks to these platforms' in-depth product descriptions, specifications, user reviews, and ratings.

Buying online also has plenty of choices, making it easy to compare features and prices between different brands and models. Online sellers often offer the ease of home delivery as well.

3) Culinary fairs

Sellers and manufacturers often display their products at these fairs, including fondue machines. You can examine various possibilities, evaluate multiple brands and models, and even see live demonstrations of how this equipment works by going.

You can directly interact with manufacturers and representatives at a trade show to learn more about the capabilities and uses of the devices.

4) Local kitchenware boutiques

These shops focus on offering distinctive, handcrafted products to a sophisticated clientele. As well as fostering a feeling of community, supporting local businesses allows you to find unusual equipment that may not be accessible through larger dealers.

5) Manufacturers' websites

Many fondue machine manufacturers have official websites where you can browse and purchase their products.

The advantage of doing so is that you could get reliable and up-to-date information about the machines sold by the company. You can review the machines' full specifications, watch how-to videos, and learn everything you need to know about them.

You can also contact customer service through the manufacturers' websites, where you can ask questions and get advice tailored to your needs. Buying directly from the manufacturer guarantees the authenticity and is often coupled with information on post-purchase and warranty support.

Chapter 3: How to plan a perfect fondue dinner

3.1 Tips and suggestions for a fondue dinner

Here, you will find the step-by-step process for providing a top-fondue dining experience.

1) Choose the type of fondue

Decide the type of fondue you want to serve: cheese, meat, or chocolate dessert. Each type requires specific tools and procedures. Consider your guests' needs and preferences and choose the most suitable option.

2) Plan the menu in every detail

Create a well-balanced menu that complements fondue:

- cheese fondue requires a series of foods to be dipped, such as vegetables, fruit, and bread;
- meat fondue is based on a careful selection of meats;
- chocolate fondue goes well with such biscuits, fruit, or marshmallows.

3) Set the table

Choose a shared dining experience by setting up a large table where everyone can gather around the fondue pot. Use a tablecloth or placemats with earth tones or warm colors to evoke a welcoming atmosphere. Ensure enough room for guests to comfortably reach the fondue pot and dipping items.

Set out individual fondue dishes for each guest and place a fork for each guest; put heat-resistant gloves near the fondue pot for safe handling. Provide bowls for dipping sauces and skimmers for removing food from the pot.

4) Take care of the environment and furnishings

Enhance the atmosphere with candles or soft lighting, which creates an intimate environment. Add themed decor or seasonal elements to suit the occasion, such as fresh flowers or rustic accents. Choose background music that fits the mood, be it relaxing tunes or upbeat melodies.

5) Prepare the fondue station

For cheese fondue, place the cheese fondue pot on a stable and heat-resistant surface.

Place the fondue burner under the pot, maintaining a safe distance from flammable materials, and place the dipping elements on a plate or cutting board near the pot.

For meat fondue, place the pot in a safe and accessible place, and adjust the fondue burner according to the type of meat you want to cook.

Give guests small saucers for cooked meat to place after dipping.

For chocolate fondue, place the saucepan on a heatproof surface. If you use a chocolate fountain, set it up on a stable base so it is level and secure.

6) Educate guests

Before you dive into the fondue experience, explain to your guests how to use fondue forks to dip and cook items, and emphasize the importance of avoiding double dipping to maintain hygiene and food safety. For meat fondue, make known the cooking times for each type of meat so that all guests can enjoy perfectly cooked morsels.

3.2 The drinks that go best with fondue

Selecting the right drink to accompany a fondue meal is vital to this culinary experience.

The ideal beverage should pair well with the flavors and textures of the fondue, thus enhancing the entire meal.

Wine

White wines are often the perfect choice for cheese fondue. A sparkling white wine with good acidity can bring out the richness of the cheese, refreshing the palate between every bite. Wines with fruity and floral notes can harmonize with the flavors of dipped ingredients.

Red wines are a standard meat fondue option. Especially wines with fruity and earthy characteristics complement the depth of flavor of the meats without overpowering them. Remember to avoid very tannic red wines that could cover the delicate flavors of the meat.

Beer

A light, sparkling beer can be a great pairing with cheese fondue.

An amber beer can be combined with meat fondues; these beers often have malted and lightly caramelized notes that can complement the flavors of cooked meats.

Alcohol-free drinks

A bottle of sparkling water can serve as a refreshing option, refreshing the palate and contrasting the savory sauces.

Non-alcoholic mocktails with fresh fruit juices and herbs can provide a valid alternative to alcoholic drinks. They can be customized to fit the fondue dinner theme better.

Herbal teas

Herbal teas such as peppermint, chamomile, or other fresh herbs can provide a contrast to the savory or sweet elements of fondue.

Tea

After the meal, offer a digestive tea like mint or ginger. These teas aid digestion and allow you to have a satisfying end to your meal.

Chapter 4: Cheese fondue recipes

1) Mixed Swiss cheese fondue

Preparation time: 40 minutes

Cooking time: 30 minutes

Number of servings: 6

Ingredients:

- 2 whole cloves of garlic
- 1 cup of white wine
- 1/2 cup lemon juice
- 14 ounces Gruyere cheese, grated
- 12 ounces Emmental cheese, grated
- 1 tablespoon cornstarch
- 1 tablespoon cherry brandy
- 2 teaspoons ground black pepper
- 1 teaspoon nutmeg
- 1 teaspoon of salt

Dippers: Apple slices, Pear slices, Crispy croutons

Preparation procedure:

Take the fondue pot and rub the bottom of the pot thoroughly with the garlic cloves.

Pour the wine, lemon juice, and cherry brandy into the pot and cook for 5 minutes. Subsequently, add the Emmental and Gruyere in this order and cook over medium heat for 25 minutes, stirring frequently.

Gently stir in the cornstarch and season with salt, black pepper, and nutmeg.

Keep the pan warm on the fondue burner, and immerse the apple slices, pear slices, and crunchy croutons.

Nutritional values (per serving):

Fat: 16.5 g - Carbohydrates: 12 g - Protein: 21g - Calories: 295

2) Cheddar cheese fondue, mustard and double malt beer

Preparation time: 25 minutes

Cooking time: 20 minutes

Number of servings: 6

Ingredients:

- 1 clove of garlic, cut in half
- 1/2 cup double malt beer
- 14 ounces sharp cheese, grated
- 12 ounces grated hard Dutch cheese
- 1 tablespoon cornstarch
- 2 teaspoons spicy mustard
- 1 teaspoon ground black pepper
- 1 teaspoon paprika powder
- 1 teaspoon of salt

Dippers: Cured sausages, Broccoli florets, Crunchy bread cubes, Carrots

Preparation procedure:

Take a fondue pot and carefully rub the bottom with a clove of garlic cut in half.

Pour the beer into the saucepan and heat over low heat for a few minutes.

Add the hard cheese to the sharp cheese and cook for about 20 minutes, until the cheese is melted; stir occasionally to keep the cheese mixture from sticking to the bottom of the pot.

Take a small bowl, pour in the cornstarch with a bit of water, and beat vigorously to form a thick paste. Stir into cheese mixture and add

spicy mustard; season with black pepper, paprika powder, and salt.

Keep the pan warm on the fondue burner, and immerse the seasoned sausages, broccoli florets, bread cubes, and baby carrots.

Nutritional values (per serving):

Fat: 24 g - Carbohydrates: 16 g - Protein: 21 g - Calories: 340

3) Cheese fondue with herbs and pine nuts

Preparation time: 25 minutes

Cooking time: 15-22 minutes

Number of servings: 4

Ingredients:

- 1 sweet onion, finely chopped
- 1/2 cup sparkling white wine
- 12 ounces of sliced herbed cheese
- 10 ounces of Emmental cheese, grated
- 2 tablespoons pine nuts
- 1 tablespoon cherry liqueur
- 1 tablespoon cornstarch
- 1 teaspoon ground black pepper

Dippers: Apple slices, Crispy bread cubes

Preparation procedure:

Place the fondue pot on the fire, pour in the wine and the sweet onion, and heat over low heat for a few minutes.

Add the Emmental cheese, herb cheese, and pine nuts, and cook for 15-22 minutes until the cheese mixture is completely smooth.

Take a small container, and pour the cornstarch and the cherry liqueur; mix well until a paste forms, and add to the pan with the melted cheese.

Season with black pepper, and keep warm on the fondue burner.

Enjoy cheese fondue with apple slices and crispy bread cubes.

Nutritional values (per serving):

Fat: 19 g - Carbohydrates: 11 g - Protein: 16 g - Calories: 265

4) Cheese fondue with bacon

Preparation time: 35 minutes

Cooking time: 30 minutes

Number of servings: 6

Ingredients:

- 6 whole slices of cooked bacon
- 1 red onion finely chopped
- 2 cups dry white wine
- 14 ounces Gruyere cheese, grated
- 14 ounces soft cheese, cut into slices
- 2 tablespoons cornstarch
- 1 teaspoon cayenne pepper

Dippers: Boiled potatoes, Sliced celery

Preparation procedure:

Place the slices of bacon, the red onion, and the white wine in the fondue pot and heat for 5 minutes, stirring with a wooden spoon.

Add the Gruyere and soft cheese, and cook over medium heat for 25 minutes until melted and smooth.

Mix the cornstarch into the pot and season with the cayenne pepper.

Keep the pan warm on the fondue burner, and immerse the boiled potatoes and celery.

Nutritional values (per serving):

Fat: 17 g - Carbohydrates: 11 g - Protein: 21 g - Calories: 335

5) Truffle cheese fondue

Preparation time: 35 minutes

Cooking time: 30 minutes

Number of servings: 6

Ingredients:

- 1 clove garlic, minced
- 1 cup of red wine
- 14 ounces thinly sliced fontina cheese
- 14 ounces provolone cheese, thinly sliced
- 1 tablespoon cornstarch

- 1 tablespoon Italian truffle oil
- 1/2 tablespoon grated truffle
- 2 teaspoons ground black pepper

Dippers: Asparagus, Mushrooms, Crispy bread croutons

Preparation procedure:

Place the chopped garlic in the fondue pot and spread it evenly. Pour the red wine into the saucepan and heat over low heat for 5 minutes.

Add the provolone and fontina cheese, and cook for 25 minutes, stirring frequently. Always ensure the cheese mixture does not stick to the bottom of the pan.

Place the cornstarch, grated truffle, and truffle oil, and season with black pepper.

Keep the pot warm on the fondue burner and delight in the asparagus, mushrooms, and croutons.

Nutritional values (per serving):

Fat: 16.5 g - Carbohydrates: 14 g - Protein: 18 g - Calories: 325

6) Feta and thyme fondue

Preparation time: 30 minutes

Cooking time: 20-25 minutes

Number of servings: 4

Ingredients:

- 1 whole clove of garlic
- 1 cup dry white wine
- 10 ounces cubed feta cheese
- 8 ounces mozzarella, cut into slices
- 1/2 tablespoon fresh oregano
- 2 teaspoons dried thyme
- 1 teaspoon black pepper

Dippers: Black olives, Cherry tomatoes, Cucumbers in vinegar

Preparation procedure:

Take a fondue pot and rub the whole garlic evenly across the bottom. Pour the white wine and heat over low heat for a few minutes.

Add the feta cheese and mozzarella and cook for 20–25 minutes, until melted.

Sprinkle the mixture with fresh oregano, dried thyme, and black pepper.

Keep the pan warm on the fondue burner and immerse the black olives, cherry tomatoes, and pickled cucumbers.

Nutritional values (per serving):

Fat: 15 g - Carbohydrates: 6 g - Protein: 110.5 g - Calories: 220

7) Mozzarella and dried tomato fondue

Preparation time: 25 minutes

Cooking time: 15-20 minutes

Number of servings: 6

Ingredients:

- 1 whole clove of garlic
- 1 sweet onion finely chopped
- 1 cup sparkling white wine
- 1/2 cup chopped sun-dried tomatoes
- 14 ounces mozzarella, sliced
- 2 tablespoons cornstarch
- 2 teaspoons of Worcestershire sauce
- 1 teaspoon ground black pepper

Dippers: Focaccia cut into cubes, thickly sliced salami, Carrots

Preparation procedure:

Rub the bottom of the fondue pot with the whole garlic; pour in the wine-chopped sweet onion; cook over low heat for a few minutes. Add the mozzarella, and cook for 15-20 minutes, until it completely melts.

Blend cornstarch with a splash of water to form a soft paste in a small bowl. Add the cheese mixture along with Worcester sauce, sun-dried tomatoes, and black pepper. Keep the pot warm on the fondue burner and immerse the focaccia cubes, salami slices, and gherkins.

Nutritional values (per serving):

Fat: 14 g - Carbohydrates: 11.5 g - Protein: 18 g - Calories: 345

8) Cheese fondue with corn and smoked paprika

Preparation time: 35 minutes

Cooking time: 25 minutes

Number of servings: 6

Ingredients:

- 1 whole clove of garlic
- 1 cup dry white wine
- 12 ounces sliced hard cheese
- 1 tablespoon steamed corn
- 1/2 tablespoon smoked paprika
- 1 teaspoon pink salt

Dippers: Pepper strips, Whole meal bread cubes, Cured sausages

Preparation procedure:

Rub the bottom of the fondue pan with the whole clove of garlic. Just pour the white wine into the pan and cook on low heat for a few minutes.

Add hard cheese and cook for 25 minutes, stirring constantly, until melted.

Place the cooked corn and smoked paprika into the cheese mixture and season with pink salt.

Keep the pot warm on the fondue stove, and immerse the strips of peppers, the seasoned sausages, and the cubes of whole meal bread.

Nutritional values (per serving):

Fat: 21 g - Carbohydrates: 13.5 g - Protein: 19 g - Calories: 360

9) Blue sheep cheese and walnut fondue

Preparation time: 35 minutes

Cooking time: 30 minutes

Number of servings: 8

Ingredients:

- 2 cloves of garlic, finely chopped

- 1 cup dry white wine
- 1/2 cup chopped walnuts
- 16 ounces sliced sheep's blue cheese
- 12 ounces of grated Emmental cheese
- 1 tablespoon cornstarch
- 2 teaspoons of walnut liqueur
- 1 teaspoon of salt

Dippers: Rye bread cubes, Apple slices, Celery sticks, Asparagus

Preparation procedure:

Take a fondue pot and rub the whole garlic cloves in the background. Pour the wine and walnut liqueur into the pan and cook over low heat for 5 minutes, stirring occasionally.

Add the sheep's blue cheese to the Emmental and cook for about 25 minutes, until melted.

Place the cornstarch and chopped walnuts in the pan and season with salt.

Keep the pot hot on the fondue stove and immerse the asparagus, celery stalks, apple slices, and rye bread cubes.

Nutritional values (per serving):

Fat: 16 g - Carbohydrates: 14.5 g - Protein: 15 g - Calories: 325

10) Goat cheese fondue and fig preserves

Preparation time: 35 minutes

Cooking time: 25 minutes

Number of servings: 6

Ingredients:

- 1 sweet onion, chopped
- 1/2 cup sparkling white wine
- 12 ounces of crumbled goat cheese
- 12 ounces grated Parmesan cheese
- 2 tablespoons of fig preserves
- 1 tablespoon mustard powder
- 1 tablespoon cherry liqueur
- 2 teaspoons ground black pepper

- 1 teaspoon pink salt

Dippers: Bread baguette cut into slices, Fresh figs, Cherries

Preparation procedure:

Add the chopped onion, cherry liqueur, and wine in a fondue pot, add the chopped onion wine, and cook over low heat for a few minutes.

Add the goat's cheese and grated parmesan to this order and cook over medium heat for 25 minutes until completely melted.

Place the fig preserves, powdered mustard, and sprinkle with black pepper and pink salt into the cheese mixture.

Keep the pot hot on the fondue burner and immerse the baguette slices, fresh figs, and cherries.

Nutritional values (per serving):

Fat: 19 g - Carbohydrates: 15 g - Protein: 18.4 g - Calories: 325

11) Cheddar cheese and cumin fondue

Preparation time: 40 minutes

Cooking time: 25-30 minutes

Number of servings: 4

Ingredients:

- 1 whole clove of garlic
- 1 red onion, chopped
- 1 cup of white wine
- 10 ounces shredded cheddar cheese
- 10 ounces shredded mozzarella
- 2 tablespoons cumin
- 1 tablespoon extra-virgin olive oil
- 1 tablespoon cornstarch
- 1 teaspoon paprika powder
- 1 teaspoon black pepper

Dippers: Celery sticks, 5-grain bread cubes, Broccoli florets

Preparation procedure:

Take a fondue pan and rub the bottom with the whole garlic clove; pour in the white wine, chopped red onion, and olive oil; and cook for 5 minutes.

Add the mozzarella and cheddar cheese, and cook for 15-20 minutes until melted and smooth.

Put the cornstarch in the pan and cook over low heat for another 5 minutes. Season with black pepper and ground paprika.

Keep the pot warm on the fondue burner.

Immerse the broccoli florets, the 5-grain bread cubes, and the celery stalks in the fondue.

Nutritional values (per serving):

Fat: 18 g - Carbohydrates: 10.5 g - Protein: 16 g - Calories: 345

12) French cheese fondue, brie, and strawberries

Preparation time: 35 minutes

Cooking time: 30 minutes

Number of servings: 8

Ingredients:

- 2 whole cloves of garlic
- 1/2 cup white wine
- 14 ounces soft French cheese, cut into slices
- 12 ounces Brie cheese, cut into cubes
- 1/2 cup strawberry jam
- 1 tablespoon cornstarch
- 2 teaspoons sea salt
- 1 teaspoon cayenne pepper

Dippers: Crispy baguette slices, Fresh strawberries

Preparation procedure:

Take the garlic cloves and rub them evenly over the bottom of the pan. Pour in the wine and cook over low heat for a few minutes.

Add the French cheese and the brie in that order, and cook for at least 25 minutes until melted.

Take a bowl and stir the cornstarch with a bit of water until a paste forms.

Place the cornstarch paste and strawberry jam in the saucepan and cook for another 5 minutes. Season with cayenne and salt.

Keep the pot warm on the fondue stove, and immerse the crispy baguette slices and the strawberries.

Nutritional values (per serving):

Fat: 14.5 g - Carbohydrates: 12 g - Protein: 21 g - Calories: 315

13) Cream cheese and spinach fondue

Preparation time: 35 minutes

Cooking time: 30 minutes

Number of servings: 4

Ingredients:

- 1 onion, chopped
- 1 cup of sparkling white wine
- 10 ounces cream cheese
- 8 ounces of Emmental cheese
- 1 cup fresh spinach
- 1/2 tablespoon vegetable broth
- 1 tablespoon cornstarch
- 1 teaspoon black pepper

Dippers: Carrots, Cucumbers, Roasted slices of bread

Preparation procedure:

Pour the white wine, the vegetable broth, and the chopped onion into a fondue pot and cook on low heat for 5 minutes. Add the Emmental cheese and cream cheese and cook for 20 minutes.

Place the spinach in the pan and cook for about 5 minutes, mixing the ingredients. Mix cornstarch with the cheese mixture and season with black pepper.

Keep the pot warm on the fondue stove, and immerse the baby carrots, cucumbers, and roasted slices of bread.

Nutritional values (per serving):

Fat: 22.5 g - Carbohydrates: 15 g - Protein: 18g - Calories: 335

14) Goat cheese fondue and pepper cream

Preparation time: 30 minutes

Cooking time: 25 minutes

Number of servings: 6

Ingredients:

- 1 whole clove of garlic
- 1 chopped red pepper
- 1 cup of red wine
- 12 ounces goat's ricotta
- 10 ounces mozzarella, sliced
- 1 tablespoon of red pepper cream
- 2 teaspoons chili powder
- 1 tablespoon cornstarch
- 1 teaspoon of salt
- 1 teaspoon black pepper

Dippers: Chicken strips, Roasted bread cubes, Radishes

Preparation procedure:

Take a fondue pan and rub the bottom evenly with the whole garlic. Pour in the red wine and the chopped red pepper, and cook for 5 minutes, stirring now and then.

Gradually add the goat's ricotta and the sliced mozzarella and cook for 20 minutes, stirring frequently until melted. Place the chili powder and the cornstarch in the pan and continue to cook for a few minutes. Season the fondue with black pepper and salt.

Keep the pan warm on the fondue burner and immerse the roasted bread cubes, chicken strips, and radishes.

Nutritional values (per serving):

Fat: 17.5 g - Carbohydrates: 12 g - Protein: 21 g - Calories: 318

15) Gruyere cheese and sweet onion fondue

Preparation time: 35 minutes

Cooking time: 20-25 minutes

Number of servings: 6

Ingredients:

- 1 sweet onion, finely chopped
- 1 cup of white wine
- 14 ounces Gruyere cheese, cut into slices
- 12 ounces of grated Emmental cheese
- 1 tablespoon butter
- 1 tablespoon cornstarch
- 1 teaspoon ground black pepper
- 1 teaspoon of salt

Dippers: Bread croutons, Sliced apple, Liver sausages

Preparation procedure:

Put the sweet onion, white wine, and butter in a fondue pan and cook over low heat for a few minutes.

Add the Emmental and Gruyere cheese and cook for 20–25 minutes, until melted and firm.

In a small bowl, blend cornstarch with a bit of white wine and water until it forms a smooth paste. Add to the cheese mixture, and season with black pepper and salt.

Keep the pan warm on the fondue burner, and immerse the croutons, sliced apple, and liver sausages.

Nutritional values (per serving):

Fat: 17 g - Carbohydrates: 14 g - Protein: 21 g - Calories: 310

16) Provolone and parmesan fondue

Preparation time: 25 minutes

Cooking time: 15-20 minutes

Number of servings: 6

Ingredients:

- 1 whole clove of garlic
- 1 cup of red wine
- 12 ounces grated provolone

- 12 ounces grated Parmesan cheese
- 1 tablespoon extra-virgin olive oil
- 1 tablespoon cornstarch
- 1 teaspoon Italian seasoning
- 1 teaspoon paprika powder

Dippers: Cherry tomatoes, Stoneless green olives, Cucumbers, Whole meal bread cubes

Preparation procedure:

Take a fondue pan and rub the bottom with the entire garlic clove. Pour the red wine into the olive oil and heat for a few minutes.

Add the grated provolone and the grated parmesan and cook, stirring frequently, for 15-20 minutes.

Mix cornstarch and Italian seasoning with cheese, and sprinkle with paprika powder.

Keep the pot on the fondue burner, and immerse the whole meal bread cubes, olives, cherry tomatoes, and cucumbers.

Nutritional values (per serving):

Fat: 21.5 g - Carbohydrates: 16 g - Protein: 23 g - Calories: 365

17) Fontina cheese fondue, minced garlic, and mushrooms

Preparation time: 30 minutes

Cooking time: 25 minutes

Number of servings: 6

Ingredients:

- 1 clove garlic, minced
- 1 cup of dry white wine
- 14 ounces fontina cheese, grated
- 10 ounces parmesan, grated
- 1 cup sliced mushrooms
- 1 tablespoon fresh parsley
- 1 tablespoon cornstarch
- 1 teaspoon black pepper

Dippers: Asparagus, Roasted bread cubes

Preparation procedure:

Take a fondue pot, pour the chopped garlic and white wine, and cook for about 5 minutes.

Add the Parmesan and fontina in this order, and cook for 20 minutes, stirring until melted and firm.

In a separate pan, cook the sliced mushrooms for a few minutes, sprinkle them with the parsley, and incorporate them into the cheese fondue. Cook on low heat for 5 minutes.

Combine the cornstarch with a bit of white wine in a small bowl to create a firm paste. Place in the pot with fondue, and season with black pepper.

Keep the pot warm on the fondue burner, and immerse the roasted bread cubes and asparagus.

Nutritional values (per serving):

Fat: 16.5 g - Carbohydrates: 12 g - Protein: 15 g - Calories: 345

18) Herb cream cheese and mozzarella fondue

Preparation time: 35 minutes

Cooking time: 30 minutes

Number of servings: 6

Ingredients:

- 1 whole clove of garlic
- 1 cup of white wine
- 14 ounces herbed cream cheese
- 12 ounces mozzarella, sliced
- 1 tablespoon fresh parsley
- 1 tablespoon dried thyme
- 1 tablespoon cornstarch
- 1 teaspoon black pepper
- 1 teaspoon of salt

Dippers: Chicken strips, Cherry tomatoes, Carrots, Whole meal bread cubes

Preparation procedure:

Take a fondue pot and rub the base with the whole garlic. Pour the wine into the saucepan and cook over low heat for a few minutes.

Add the mozzarella and cream cheese in this order and cook for 25 minutes, stirring well, until it becomes smooth and compact.

Place the parsley, thyme, and corn starch in the pan and drain; cook for 5 minutes; scatter with black pepper and salt.

Keep the pan on the fondue burner and immerse the baby carrots, tomatoes, and whole meal bread cubes.

Nutritional values (per serving):

Fat: 15 g Carbohydrates: 12 g Protein: 18 g Calories: 290

19) Gorgonzola cheese fondue, walnuts and pears

Preparation time: 30 minutes

Cooking time: 25 minutes

Number of servings: 6

Ingredients:

- 1 large pear, cut into slices
- 1 cup of white wine
- 12 ounces shredded Gorgonzola cheese
- 12 ounces of Emmental cheese, sliced
- 1 tablespoon chopped walnuts
- 1 tablespoon garlic powder
- 1/2 tablespoon cornstarch
- 2 teaspoons of honey
- 1 teaspoon nutmeg
- 1 teaspoon of salt

Dippers: Celery sticks, Roasted bread cubes, Pear slices

Preparation procedure:

Take a fondue pot, pour in the white wine garlic powder, and cook over a low flame for a few minutes.

Add the Gorgonzola and Emmental cheese and cook over medium heat for 20 minutes. Place the cornstarch, chopped walnuts, pear slices, and honey in the pan and cook for another 5 minutes.

Keep the pan warm on the fondue burner and immerse the roasted bread cubes, celery sticks, and pear slices.

Nutritional values (per serving):

Fat: 19 g - Carbohydrates: 12 g - Protein: 16.5 g - Calories: 320

20) Fondue with sheep's ricotta, mozzarella and caramelized apples

Preparation time: 30 minutes

Cooking time: 15-20 minutes

Number of servings: 8

Ingredients:

- 3 cored apples cut into slices
- 1 whole clove of garlic
- 1 cup dry white wine
- 14 ounces sheep's milk ricotta
- 14 ounces mozzarella, sliced
- 2 tablespoons peanut butter
- 1 tablespoon cornstarch
- 2 teaspoons paprika powder
- 1 teaspoon of salt

Dippers: Raisin croutons, Chicken sausages, Celery sticks

Preparation procedure:

Take a fondue pan and evenly sprinkle the bottom with the garlic clove; pour the wine and heat for a few minutes, stirring well.

Add the sheep's ricotta to the mozzarella, and cook for 15-20 minutes until they are compacted.

Mix cornstarch, apple slices, peanut butter, and paprika powder into the cheese mixture and sprinkle with salt.

Keep the pan warm on the fondue burner, and dip the raisin croutons, chicken sausages, and celery sticks.

Nutritional values (per serving):

Fat: 17 g - Carbohydrates: 16.5 g - Protein: 22 g - Calories: 320

21) Classic Valdo stan fondue

Preparation Time: 30 minutes

Cooking Time: 15 minutes

Number of Servings: 4 / 6

Ingredients:

- 1 lb. fresh fontina cheese from Valle d'Aosta made into small pieces
- 1 1/2 ounces of butter
- 1 pinch of ground white pepper
- 1 cup of whole milk
- 5 egg yolks

Dippers: Slices of toasted bread

Preparation Procedure:

Get the fondue pot, pour the chopped fontina cheese, milk, and butter, and put it on low heat for 15 minutes.

Using a whisk, stir continuously until the cheese has completely melted. Then add the egg yolks and continue simmering until the mixture becomes smooth and creamy.

Using fondue forks, stab slices of toasted bread into the fondue for a few seconds and enjoy.

Nutritional Values (per serving):

Fats: 32g - Carbohydrates: 21g - Proteins: 24g - Calories: 340

22) Fontina fondue with sausage and bread croutons

Preparation Time: 28 minutes

Cooking Time: 15 minutes

Number of Servings: 4 / 6

Ingredients:

- 1 lb. chopped fontina cheese
- 4 sausages
- 4 egg yolks
- 2 cups whole milk
- Cassette toasted bread cut into small pieces
- 1/4 cup dry white wine
- 1/3 cup butter

Dippers: Slices of toasted bread

Preparation Procedure:

Get a frying pan, and after piercing the sausages, put them in the pan and cook them for about 15 minutes over low heat, deglazing with white wine.

Take the fondue pot, put the fontina cheese, milk, and butter on low heat, and stir until the cheese has melted. Then, add the egg yolks and continue stirring until the mixture is smooth and homogeneous.

Cut the sausages into pieces and place them on a plate.

Using fondue forks, pierce the pieces of sausage and bread, dip them in the fondue for a few seconds, and enjoy.

Nutritional Values (per serving):

Fats: 30g - Carbohydrates: 20g - Proteins: 18g - Calories: 358

23) Fontina fondue with beef patties and bread croutons

Preparation Time: 30 minutes

Cooking Time: 15-20 minutes

Number of Servings: 4 / 6

Ingredients:

- 1 lb. chopped fontina cheese
- 20 beef patties
- 4 egg yolks

- 2 cups whole milk
- Toasted cassette bread cut into small pieces
- 1/4 cup dry white wine
- 1/3 cup butter

Dippers: Slices of toasted bread

Preparation Procedure:

Get a frying pan, put the patties in, and cook them for 15-20 minutes over low heat, deglazing with white wine.

Take the fondue pot and put the fontina cheese, milk, and butter over low heat. Stir until the cheese has melted. Now add the egg yolks and keep stirring until the mixture is smooth and homogeneous.

Arrange the cooked patties on a plate.

Using fondue forks, pierce the patties and bread pieces, dip them in the fondue for a few seconds, and enjoy.

Nutritional Values (per serving):

Fats: 28g - Carbohydrates: 16g - Proteins: 15g - Calories: 312

24) Emmenthal and groovier fondue with fish patties

Preparation Time: 20 minutes

Cooking Time: 15 minutes

Number of Servings: 4 / 6

Ingredients:

- 1 lb. shredded Emmenthal
- 1 lb. chopped groovier
- 25 fish patties
- 1 egg yolks
- 1 cup whole milk
- Crusty toasted bread cut into small pieces
- 1/4 cup dry white wine
- 1/4 cup butter

Dippers: Slices of toasted bread

Preparation Procedure:

Get a frying pan, put in the fish patties, and cook them for 15 minutes on low heat, deglazing with white wine.

Take the fondue pot and put the chopped Emmenthal, chopped groovier, milk, and butter over low heat and stir until the cheese has melted. Add the egg yolk and continue stirring until the mixture is smooth and homogeneous.

Arrange the cooked patties on a plate.

Using fondue forks, pierce the patties and bread pieces, dip them in the fondue for a few seconds, and enjoy.

Nutritional Values (per serving):

Fats: 18g - Carbohydrates: 16g - Proteins: 15g - Calories: 287

25) Fontina fondue with Wurstels, mixed vegetables and bread croutons

Preparation Time: 25 minutes

Cooking Time: 15 minutes

Number of Servings: 4

Ingredients:

- 1 lb. chopped fontina cheese
- 4 wurstels made into pieces
- 1 egg yolk
- 1 cup whole milk
- Toasted bread cut into small pieces
- 1/3 cup butter

Dippers: Blanched mixed vegetables

Preparation Procedure:

Get a frying pan, put the chopped frankfurters in the pan, and cook them for 15 minutes on low heat until they are well roasted.

Get the fondue pot, put the fontina cheese, milk, and butter on low heat, and stir until the cheese has melted. At this point, add the egg yolk and keep stirring until the mixture is smooth and homogeneous.

Using fondue forks, pierce the sausage pieces, vegetables, and bread, dip them in the fondue for a few seconds, and enjoy.

Nutritional Values (per serving):

Fats: 26g - Carbohydrates: 14g - Proteins: 21g - Calories: 330

26) Cheese fondue with new potatoes and crispy bread croutons

Preparation Time: 25 minutes

Cooking Time: 15-20 minutes

Number of Servings: 4

Ingredients:

- 1 lb. shredded fontina cheese
- 1 lb. shredded Emmenthal
- 1 lb. washed and blanched new potatoes with all their skins on
- 1 egg yolk
- 1 cup of whole milk
- 1/3 cup butter

Dippers: Toasted bread cut into small pieces

Preparation Procedure:

Get the fondue pot and put the fontina cheese, milk and butter on low heat and stir for 15-20 minutes, until the cheese has melted. At this point add the egg yolk and keep stirring until the mixture is smooth and homogeneous.

Using fondue forks, pierce the blanched new potatoes and bread, dip them in the fondue for a few seconds and enjoy.

Nutritional Values (per serving):

Fats: 26g - Carbohydrates: 18g - Proteins: 21g - Calories: 360

27) Cheese fondue with roast ham, vegetables and crispy bread croutons

Preparation Time: 25 minutes

Cooking Time: 15 minutes

Number of Servings: 4

Ingredients:

- 1 lb. chopped Fontina cheese
- 1 lb. shredded Emmenthal cheese
- 2 lb. roast ham
- 1 egg yolk
- 1 cup whole milk
- 1/3 cup butter
- Sliced crusty bread

Dippers: Blanched mixed vegetables

Preparation Procedure:

Get a nonstick skillet and cook the roast ham until it is well cooked and toasted, about 15 minutes.

Get the fondue pot, put the fontina cheese, milk, and butter on low heat, and stir until the cheese has melted. Add the egg yolk and continue stirring until the mixture is smooth and homogeneous.

Pierce the toasted roast ham, mixed vegetables, and bread using fondue forks, dip them in the fondue for a few seconds, and enjoy.

Nutritional Values (per serving):

Fats: 19g - Carbohydrates: 22g - Proteins: 18g - Calories: 390

Chapter 5: Oil fondue recipes

1) Beef Fondue

Preparation Time: 28 minutes

Cooking Time: 5-6 minutes

Number of Servings: 4

Ingredients:

- 2 lb. of beef sirloin, cut into small pieces
- 6 - 8 cups of Fondue Oil (vegetable, seed or peanut oil), whichever you prefer
- Garlic aioli dipping sauce to taste
- Teriyaki dipping sauce to taste
- Horseradish dipping sauce to taste

Dippers: Vegetables, bread cubes and mushrooms

Preparation Procedure:

Warm the oil in the fondue pot to 380°F.

Get the beef slices with fondue forks and cook them in the hot oil for 5–6 minutes until the desired doneness. Dip the cooked beef into the sauces and enjoy with the bread cubes, vegetables, and mushrooms.

Nutritional Values (per serving):

Fats: 28g - Carbohydrates: 3g - Proteins: 46g - Calories: 220

2) Fondue with scallops and red shrimp

Preparation Time: 30 minutes

Cooking time: 2 minutes

Number of Servings: 4

Ingredients:

- 1 lb. red shrimp, peeled and deveined
- 6 – 8 cups fondue oil (canola, seed or peanut)
- 1 lb. scallops
- Garlic butter sauce for dipping to taste

Dippers: Bread cubes and assorted vegetables to taste

Preparation Procedure:

Warm the oil in the fondue pot to 360°F.

Get the shrimp and scallops with fondue forks and cook them in the hot oil for about 2 minutes until the desired doneness.

Dip the cooked seafood into the garlic butter sauce and enjoy with bread cubes and mixed vegetables.

Nutritional Values (per serving):

Fats: 35g - Carbohydrates: 6g - Proteins: 68g - Calories: 242

3) Fondue of vegetables

Preparation Time: 20 minutes

Cooking Time: 2 – 3 minutes

Number of Servings: 4

Ingredients:

- 2 lb. assorted vegetables (broccoli florets, bell pepper strips, carrot sticks, cherry tomatoes)
- 6 – 8 cups fondue oil (canola, seed or peanut)
- Creamy herb-based dipping sauce

Dippers: Bread cubes and assorted vegetables to taste

Preparation Procedure:

Warm the oil in the 360° fondue pot. Get the vegetables with the fondue forks and cook them in the hot oil for about 2 to 3 minutes until they are cooked to the desired degree. Dip the cooked vegetables into the creamy herb sauce.

Nutritional Values (per serving):

Fats: 6g - Carbohydrates: 9g - Proteins: 18g - Calories: 78

4) Chicken fondue and pineapple

Preparation Time: 25 minutes

Cooking time: 4 – 5 minutes

Number of Servings: 4

Ingredients:

- 2 lb. boneless chicken breast, cut into pieces
- 6 - 8 cups fondue oil (canola, seed or peanut)
- 1 Fresh pineapple cleaned and cut into small pieces
- Dipping sauce for dipping sweet to taste
- Dipping sauce for spicy gravy to taste

Dippers: Bread cubes and assorted vegetables to taste

Preparation Procedure:

Warm the oil in the fondue pot to 370°.

Get the chicken, pineapple, bread, and vegetables with fondue forks and cook them in the hot oil for about 4 to 5 minutes, until desired doneness.

Dip in the sweet and hot sauce.

Nutritional Values (per serving):

Fats: 12g - Carbohydrates: 19g - Proteins: 65g - Calories: 190

5) Thai spicy fondue

Preparation Time: 32 minutes

Cooking Time: 5 – 6 minutes

Number of Servings: 4

Ingredients:

- 1/2 lb. beef cut into thin pieces
- 1/2 lb. chicken cut into thin pieces
- 6 – 8 cups fondue oil (canola, seed or peanut)
- 1/2 lb. tofu cut into thin pieces

- Spicy peanut dipping sauce to taste
- Sweet butter dipping sauce to taste

Dippers: Rice noodles and mixed vegetables

Preparation Procedure:

Warm the oil in the fondue pot to 380°F.

Get the beef, chicken, tofu, and vegetables with fondue forks and cook them in the hot oil for about 5–6 minutes, until the desired degree of doneness.

Dip them in the sauces and serve with rice noodles.

Nutritional Values (per serving):

Fats: 22g - Carbohydrates: 16g - Proteins: 48g - Calories: 186

6) Fondue of turkey with bread and vegetables

Preparation Time: 20 minutes

Cooking Time: 4 – 5 minutes

Number of Servings: 4

Ingredients:

- 2 lb. turkey boneless and cut into small pieces
- 6 - 8 cups fondue oil (canola, seed or peanut)
- Mayonnaise dipping sauce to taste
- Mustard dipping sauce to taste

Dippers: Bread cubes, broccoli and cauliflower

Preparation Procedure:

Warm the oil in the fondue pot to 350°F.

Get the turkey, bread, broccoli, and cauliflower with fondue forks and cook them in the hot oil for about 4 to 5 minutes, until desired doneness.

Dip them in the mayonnaise and mustard sauces and enjoy.

Nutritional Values (per serving):

Fats: 23g - Carbohydrates: 11g - Proteins: 39g - Calories: 223

7) Seafood and fish fondue

Preparation Time: 25 minutes

Cooking time: 2 minutes

Number of Servings: 4

Ingredients:

- 1 lb. red shrimp, cleaned and peeled
- 1 lb. of scallops
- 1 lb. sea bream or sea bass filleted and cut into small pieces
- 6 – 8 cups fondue oil (canola, seed or peanut)
- Lemon-butter dipping sauce

Dippers: 2 Baguette slices - asparagus cleaned and chopped

Preparation Procedure:

Warm the oil in the fondue pot to 340°F.

Get the seafood, fish chunks, bread, and asparagus chunks with fondue forks and cook them in the hot oil for about 2 minutes, until cooked. Then dip them into the sauce and enjoy.

Nutritional Values (per serving):

Fats: 18g - Carbohydrates: 9g - Proteins: 36g - Calories: 160

8) Herb fondue

Preparation Time: 25 minutes

Cooking time: 2 minutes

Number of Servings: 4

Ingredients:

- 1 bunch of washed and dried fresh herbs (rosemary, thyme, oregano)
- Balsamic vinegar and olive oil dipping sauce to taste
- 6 – 8 cups fondue oil (canola, seed or peanut)

Dippers: Sliced artisan bread, cherry tomatoes and olives

Preparation Procedure:

Infuse the oil with fresh herbs in the fondue pot by heating it to 300°F until fragrant.

Get the bread, tomatoes, and olives with fondue forks and dip them in the herb-infused oil for about 2 minutes. Dip them in the balsamic oil sauce and enjoy.

Nutritional Values (per serving):

Fats: 12g - Carbohydrates: 39g - Proteins: 15g - Calories: 96

9) Asian tofu and mixed Asian vegetable fondue

Preparation Time: 25 minutes

Cooking Time: 2 minutes

Number of Servings: 4

Ingredients:

- 2 lb. tofu, sliced
- 6 – 8 cups fondue oil (canola, seed or peanut)
- Ginger and soy dipping sauce

Dippers: 1 lb. of Bok choy - 1 lb. of bell peppers, sliced into strips

Preparation Procedure:

Warm the oil in the fondue pot to 355°F.

Get the tofu pieces, Bok choy, and chopped peppers with fondue forks and cook them in the hot oil for about 2 minutes, until cooked. Dip them in the sauce and enjoy.

Nutritional Values (per serving):

Fats: 9g - Carbohydrates: 2g - Proteins: 36g - Calories: 152

10) Fondue of mozzarella cheese, cherry tomatoes and breadsticks

Preparation Time: 20 minutes

Cooking Time: 1 minute

Number of Servings: 4

Ingredients:

- 2 lb. breadsticks
- Tomato and spicy mustard dipping sauces
- 6 – 8 cups fondue oil (canola, seed or peanut)

Dippers: Cherry tomatoes and mozzarella balls

Preparation Procedure:

Warm the oil in the fondue pot to 340°F. Dip the breadsticks into the hot oil until crispy.

Using fondue forks, take the tomatoes and mozzarella balls and dip them in the hot oil for about 1 minute. Dip them in the sauce along with the breadsticks and enjoy.

Nutritional Values (per serving):

Fats: 12g - Carbohydrates: 56g - Proteins: 28g - Calories: 218

11) Fondue with tortillas and vegetable sticks

Preparation Time: 20 minutes

Cooking time: 1 – 2 minutes

Number of Servings: 4

Ingredients:

- 6 – 8 cups fondue oil (canola, seed or peanut)
- Nacho cheese sauce to taste
- Guacamole dipping sauce to taste

Dippers: Tortilla chips and vegetable sticks

Preparation Procedure:

Warm the oil in the fondue pot to 340°F. Dip the tortilla chips and vegetable sticks into the hot oil for 1 to 2 minutes until the vegetables are cooked. Dip them in the sauces and enjoy.

Nutritional Values (per serving):

Fats: 15g - Carbohydrates: 22g - Proteins: 35g - Calories: 145

12) Chicken teriyaki fondue

Preparation Time: 25 minutes

Cooking Time: 2 – 3 minutes

Number of Servings: 4

Ingredients:

- 2 lb. boneless chicken thighs, cut into small pieces
- 6 – 8 cups fondue oil (canola, seed or peanut)
- Teriyaki sauce to taste
- Sesame sauce to taste

Dippers: Pineapple chunks and zucchini strips

Preparation Procedure:

Marinate chicken in teriyaki sauce for 20 minutes. Warm the oil in the fondue pot to 355°F.

Stick the chicken in the fondue forks and cook in the oil for 2-3 minutes. Dip the chicken, pineapple, and zucchini into the sesame sauce.

Nutritional Values (per serving):

Fats: 18g - Carbohydrates: 9g - Proteins: 38g - Calories: 225

13) Fondue of mixed seafood

Preparation Time: 36 minutes

Cooking Time: 2 – 3 minutes

Number of Servings: 4

Ingredients:

- 1 lb. squid cleaned and shredded
- 1 lb. cleaned and peeled shrimp
- 1 lb. cleaned and shelled mussels
- 6 – 8 cups fondue oil (canola, seed or peanut)
- Mayonnaise sauce for dipping

Dippers: Artichoke hearts and crusty bread

Preparation Procedure:

Warm the oil in the fondue pot to 320°F.

Using fondue forks, take the squid, shelled mussels, shrimp, artichokes, and bread and dip them in the hot oil for 2-3 minutes until cooked. Then dip the seafood and artichoke hearts in the mayonnaise sauce and enjoy.

Nutritional Values (per serving):

Fats: 15g - Carbohydrates: 32g - Proteins: 78g - Calories: 265

14) Fondue with shrimp and Cajun sausage

Preparation Time: 30 minutes

Cooking Time: 2 – 3 minutes

Number of Servings: 4

Ingredients:

- 1 lb. large shrimp, shelled and cleaned
- 6 – 8 cups fondue oil (canola, seed or peanut)
- 1 lb. pork sausage, sliced
- Sauce Remoulade for dipping
- Cajun Seasoning Sauce

Dippers: Cubes of cornbread and okra

Preparation Procedure:

Drizzle the shrimp and sausage with Cajun seasoning. Heat oil in fondue pot to 360°F.

Stick shrimp and sausage into fondue forks and cook for 2–3 minutes. Dip the cooked pieces into the remoulade sauce, cornbread cubes, and okra.

Nutritional Values (per serving):

Fats: 64g - Carbohydrates: 9g - Proteins: 38g - Calories: 275

15) Marinated chicken fondue and crispy asparagus

Preparation Time: 32 minutes

Cooking Time: 3 minutes

Number of Servings: 4

Ingredients:

- 2 lb. chicken breast, cut into slices
- 1/2 cup of herb and lemon marinade
- Garlic mayonnaise
- 6 – 8 cups fondue oil (canola, seed or peanut)

Dippers: Asparagus and lemon wedges

Preparation Procedure:

Get the chicken and marinate it for about 20 minutes in the herb and lemon marinade.

Heat oil in fondue pot to 355°F. With fondue forks, take the chicken and asparagus and cook them in the oil for about 3 minutes. Dip the chicken and asparagus into the garlic mayonnaise and enjoy.

Nutritional Values (per serving):

Fats: 9g - Carbohydrates: 12g - Proteins: 85g - Calories: 96

16) Exotic fruit fondue and almond butter cookies

Preparation Time: 30 minutes

Cooking time: a few seconds

Number of Servings: 4

Ingredients:

- 2 lb. clean and washed assorted exotic fruits (mango, papaya, kiwi)
- Chocolate dipping sauce
- 6 – 8 cups fondue oil (canola, seed or peanut)

Dippers: Butter cookies and shelled almonds

Preparation Procedure:

Warm the oil in the fondue pot to 330°F. Stab the fruits with fondue forks and dip them in the hot oil for a few seconds. Dip the fruits into the coconut chocolate sauce, butter cookies, and shelled almonds.

Nutritional Values (per serving):

Fats: 12g - Carbohydrates: 15g - Proteins: 46g - Calories: 195

17) Double fondue mushroom and cheese bread

Preparation Time: 32 minutes

Cooking time: 2 minutes

Number of Servings: 4

Ingredients:

- 2 lb. assorted mushrooms (button, cremini, shiitake)
- 2 cups Gruyere and cheddar cheese made into small pieces
- 6 – 8 cups fondue oil (canola, seed or peanut)
- 2 glasses of white wine

Dippers: Crispy bread cubes and steamed broccoli

Preparation Procedure:

Prepare the cheese in a fondue pot by melting the cheese with white wine until creamy. Warm the oil in another fondue pot to 340°F. Using fondue forks, pierce the mushrooms and cook them in the hot oil for about 2 minutes, until tender. Dip the mushrooms, bread, and broccoli into the cheese fondue and enjoy.

Nutritional Values (per serving):

Fats: 35g - Carbohydrates: 16g - Proteins: 48g - Calories: 296

18) Marinated beef fondue, peppers and crispy onions

Preparation Time: 25 minutes

Cooking time: 4 – 5 minutes

Number of Servings: 4

Ingredients:

- 2 lb. of beef sirloin, diced
- 1/2 cup lime marinade, cumin and paprika powder
- 6 – 8 cups fondue oil (canola, seed or peanut)
- Barbecue sauce to taste
- Mayonnaise garlic sauce to taste

Dippers: Strips of bell pepper and red onion wedges

Preparation Procedure:

Marinate the beef in the marinade for about 20 minutes. Warm the oil in the fondue pot to 355°F.

Using fondue forks, thread beef, bell pepper, and onion, cook for 4-5 minutes. Then dip in barbecue sauces and garlic mayonnaise and enjoy.

Nutritional Values (per serving):

Fats: 32g - Carbohydrates: 16g - Proteins: 98g - Calories: 274

19) Fruit fondue with hazelnut cream and marshmallows

Preparation Time: 20 minutes

Cooking time: a few seconds

Number of Servings: 4

Ingredients:

- 1 lb. of strawberries cleaned and cut in half
- 6 – 8 cups fondue oil (canola, seed or peanut)
- 1 lb. bananas made into rounds
- 1 cup hazelnut spreadable cream

Dippers: 1 lb. of marshmallows

Preparation Procedure:

Melt the hazelnut cream slightly in a separate saucepan.

Warm the oil in the fondue pot to 320°F.

Pierce the fruit with fondue forks and dip them into the hot oil for a few seconds, then into the hazelnut cream along with the marshmallows, and enjoy.

Nutritional Values (per serving):

Fats: 28g - Carbohydrates: 35g - Proteins: 52g - Calories: 198

20) Pork belly fondue and mixed vegetables

Preparation Time: 38 minutes

Cooking Time: 3-4 minutes

Number of Servings: 4

Ingredients:

- 2 lb. pork belly, cut into small pieces
- 6 – 8 cups fondue oil (canola, seed or peanut)
- Mayonnaise sauce to taste
- Barbecue sauce to taste

Dippers: 1 lb. chopped mixed vegetables (broccoli, carrots, onions, spinach leaves)

Preparation Procedure:

Warm the oil in the fondue pot to 360°F.

Get the pork and vegetables with fondue forks and cook them in the hot oil for 3 to 4 minutes until the desired doneness.

Dip the pork and vegetables in the sauces and enjoy.

Nutritional Values (per serving):

Fats: 56g - Carbohydrates: 5g - Proteins: 38g - Calories: 259

21) Marinated lamb fondue with soy and rosemary

Preparation Time: 45 minutes

Cooking Time: 5-8 minutes

Number of Servings: 4

Ingredients:

- 2 lb. lamb, cut into small pieces
- 1 bunch of rosemary
- 1 cup of soy sauce
- 6 – 8 cups fondue oil (canola, seed or peanut)
- Barbecue sauce to taste
- Chili sauce to taste

Dippers: Sliced champignon mushrooms and bread cubes

Preparation Procedure:

Heat oil in fondue pot to 370°F. Take a bowl, combine the soy sauce with the rosemary sprigs, and create a marinade. Dip the lamb meat into the soy and rosemary marinade for a few minutes.

Get the lamb meat, mushrooms, and bread cubes with fondue forks and cook them in the hot oil for about 5 to 8 minutes until they are cooked to the desired doneness.

Then dip into the sauces and enjoy to taste.

Nutritional Values (per serving):

Fats: 66g - Carbohydrates: 7g - Proteins: 37g - Calories: 241

22) Fondue with squid and potatoes in spicy mayonnaise

Preparation Time: 36 minutes

Cooking Time: 3-4 minutes

Number of Servings: 4

Ingredients:

- 2 lb. squid, cut into small pieces
- 6 - 8 cups fondue oil (canola, seed or peanut)
- Salsa aioli to taste
- Spicy mayonnaise sauce to taste

Dippers: Chopped potatoes blanched in water

Preparation Procedure:

Warm the oil in the fondue pot to 330°F.

Get the squid with fondue forks and cook them in the hot oil for 3 to 4 minutes until they reach the desired doneness. Then dip into the sauces along with the potatoes and enjoy the taste.

Nutritional Values (per serving):

Fats: 18g - Carbohydrates: 3g - Proteins: 69g - Calories: 148

23) Fondue Bagna Cauda of Piedmont

Preparation Time: 42 minutes

Cooking Time: 12 minutes

Number of Servings: 4 / 6

Ingredients:

- 1 cup of olive oil
- 1 carrot cut into small pieces
- 4 tbsp. butter
- 4 cloves of garlic, finely chopped
- 10 anchovy fillets, chopped
- 1 fennel cut into small pieces
- 1 cucumber chopped into small pieces
- 1 onion, chopped
- 1 lb. crusty bread cut into fine pieces
- 1 celery, chopped
- 1/2 small broccoli cut into pieces

Dippers: Mixed vegetables and pieces of crusty bread

Preparation Procedure:

Get a large pot and blend oil, butter, anchovies, and garlic with a food processor until creamy and smooth. Place on the stove and simmer for about 12 minutes, stirring everything together.

Pour everything into the fondue pot and place the pot on the fondue stove to keep it warm.

With fondue forks, pierce the vegetables and crusty bread dip for a few seconds in the fondue and enjoy.

Nutritional Values (per serving):

Fats: 48g - Carbohydrates: 36g - Proteins: 54g - Calories: 246

24) Surimi and vegetable fondue with spicy mayonnaise and crispy bread croutons

Preparation Time: 38 minutes

Cooking Time: 3-4 minutes

Number of Servings: 4

Ingredients:

- 2 lb. of surimi sticks
- 6 - 8 cups fondue oil (canola, seed or peanut)
- Salsa aioli to taste
- Spicy mayonnaise sauce to taste
- Soy sauce
- Crispy bread croutons

Dippers: Chopped cucumbers and carrots

Preparation Procedure:

Warm the oil in the fondue pot to 330°F.

Get the surimi sticks, vegetables, and bread croutons with fondue forks and cook them in the hot oil for about 3 to 4 minutes until they reach the desired doneness.

Then dip them in the sauces together to taste and enjoy.

Nutritional Values (per serving):

Fats: 58g - Carbohydrates: 34g - Proteins: 89g - Calories: 198

25) Fondue with mussels and vegetables with spicy mayonnaise and crispy bread croutons

Preparation Time: 45 minutes

Cooking Time: 5 - 6 minutes

Number of Servings: 4

Ingredients:

- 2 lb. raw open, cleaned and shelled mussels
- 6 - 8 cups fondue oil (canola, seed or peanut)
- Salsa aioli to taste
- Spicy mayonnaise sauce to taste
- Soy sauce
- Crispy bread croutons
- Cleaned blanched asparagus

Dippers: Cleaned blanched asparagus

Preparation Procedure:

Warm the oil in the fondue pot to 350° F.

Get the mussels, vegetables, and bread croutons with fondue forks and cook them in the hot oil for about 5 to 6 minutes until they reach the desired doneness.

Then dip them in the sauces to taste and enjoy.

Nutritional Values (per serving):

Fats: 38g - Carbohydrates: 34g - Proteins: 59g - Calories: 228

26) Fondue with sea bream fillet and potatoes in soy sauce

Preparation Time: 41 minutes

Cooking Time: 6 - 7 minutes

Number of Servings: 4

Ingredients:

- 2 lb. sea bream fillet, cleaned and cut into small pieces
- 6 - 8 cups fondue oil (canola, seed or peanut)
- Soy sauce
- Crispy bread croutons

Dippers: Cleaned and blanched carrots and potatoes

Preparation Procedure:

Warm the oil in the fondue pot to 340°F.

Get the filleted sea bream pieces, vegetables, and bread croutons with fondue forks and cook them in the hot oil for about 6 to 7 minutes, until they reach the desired doneness.

Then dip them in the sauces to taste and enjoy.

Nutritional Values (per serving):

Fats: 48g - Carbohydrates: 56g - Proteins: 67g - Calories: 246

27) Fondue with small pork sausages and broccoli stems and florets

Preparation Time: 29 minutes

Cooking Time: 10 - 12 minutes

Number of Servings: 4

Ingredients:

- 2 lb. small pork sausages
- 6 - 8 cups fondue oil (canola, seed or peanut)
- Barbecue sauce
- Crispy bread croutons

Dippers: Broccoli leaves and florets

Preparation Procedure:

Warm the oil in the fondue pot to 340°F.

Get the small sausages, vegetables, and bread croutons with fondue forks and cook them in the hot oil for about 10 to 12 minutes, until they reach the desired doneness.

Then dip them in the sauces to taste and enjoy.

Nutritional Values (per serving):

Fats: 64g - Carbohydrates: 38g - Proteins: 86g - Calories: 286

28) Fondue with marinated wild boar stew

Preparation Time: 30 minutes

Cooking Time: 8 - 9 minutes

Number of Servings: 4

Ingredients:

- 2 lb. wild boar stew
- 1/2 cup soy sauce
- 1 bunch of thyme
- 6 - 8 cups fondue oil (canola, seed or peanut)
- Crispy bread croutons

Dippers: Boiled mixed vegetables to taste

Preparation Procedure:

Mix the soy sauce and thyme in a bowl and mix.

Marinate the boar stew in the resulting soy sauce. Drain and set aside. Warm the oil in the fondue pot to 360°F.

Get the marinated wild boar stew, vegetables, and bread croutons with fondue forks and cook them in the hot oil for about 8 to 9 minutes until the desired cooking time is reached, and enjoy.

Nutritional Values (per serving):

Fats: 48g - Carbohydrates: 56g - Proteins: 45g - Calories: 225

29) Fondue of marinated brussels sprouts

Preparation Time: 20 minutes

Cooking Time: 10 minutes

Number of Servings: 4

Ingredients:

- 2 lb. cleaned and blanched brussels sprouts
- 1/2 cup soy sauce
- 1 bunch of chopped fresh cilantro

- 6 - 8 cups fondue oil (canola, seed or peanut)
- Spicy mayonnaise sauce

Dippers: Crispy bread croutons

Preparation Procedure:

In a bowl, pour the soy sauce and cilantro and mix.

Marinate the brussels sprouts in the resulting soy marinade. Drain and set aside.

Warm the oil in the fondue pot to 330°F.

Get the marinated brussels sprouts and the bread croutons with fondue forks and cook them in the hot oil for about 10 minutes, until the desired cooking time is reached, and enjoy by dipping in the spicy mayonnaise.

Nutritional Values (per serving):

Fats: 24g - Carbohydrates: 56g - Proteins: 36g - Calories: 174

30) Fondue with turkey stew marinated in apple cider vinegar

Preparation Time: 29 minutes

Cooking Time: 8 - 9 minutes

Number of Servings: 4

Ingredients:

- 2 lb. turkey stew
- 1/2 cup apple cider vinegar
- 1 tbsp. olive oil
- 1 bunch of chopped fresh cilantro
- 6 - 8 cups fondue oil (canola, seed or peanut)
- Spicy mayonnaise sauce
- Toasted crusty bread

Dippers: 1 chopped celery, 1 chopped cucumber, Cherry tomatoes

Preparation Procedure:

In a bowl, pour the apple cider vinegar, oil, and chopped cilantro and mix, creating a marinade.

Dip the stew in the resulting marinade for a few minutes. Drain and set aside. Warm the oil in the fondue pot to 340° F.

Get the marinated turkey stew, and the bread croutons with fondue forks and cook them in the hot oil for about 8 to 9 minutes, until the desired cooking time is reached and enjoy by dipping them along with the vegetables in the spicy mayonnaise.

Nutritional Values (per serving):

Fats: 56g - Carbohydrates: 47g - Proteins: 96g - Calories: 215

31) Fondue with lobster, potatoes, and crispy bread croutons

Preparation Time: 34 minutes

Cooking Time: 10 - 12 minutes

Number of Servings: 4

Ingredients:

- 2 lb. lobster
- 6 - 8 cups fondue oil (canola, seed or peanut)
- Spicy mayonnaise sauce
- Crispy toasted bread croutons

Dippers: Shredded blanched potatoes

Preparation Procedure:

Get a pot, fill it with water, and bring it to a boil. Pour in the lobster and blanch for a few minutes, about 4 to 5 minutes. Drain the lobster from the water and let it cool for a few minutes. Get the lobster once cold, clean it from the carapace, and chop the flesh into pieces.

Warm the oil in the fondue pot to 340°F. Get the lobster flesh pieces and bread croutons with fondue forks and cook them in the hot oil for about 6 to 7 minutes until they are cooked to the desired doneness. Then dip them into the sauce along with the potatoes and enjoy.

Nutritional Values (per serving):

Fats: 34g - Carbohydrates: 22g - Proteins: 18g - Calories: 250

Chapter 6: Broth fondue recipes

1) Beef tenderloin and sirloin fondue

Preparation Time: 20 minutes

Cooking Time: 5 – 10 minutes

Number of Servings: 4

Ingredients:

- 2 lb. beef, tenderloin or sirloin, thinly sliced
- 1 tablespoon vegetable oil
- 6 cups beef stock
- 2 cloves of garlic, finely chopped
- 2 onions, thinly sliced
- Assorted dipping sauces to taste (soy sauce, horseradish, mustard)

Preparation Procedure:

Warm vegetable oil in a fondue pot. Fry the garlic and onion until fragrant.

Add the beef stock to the pot and bring it to a boil.

Pierce the beef with fondue forks and cook in the broth over low heat until desired doneness, about 5–10 minutes, depending on taste. Then, dip the meat in the sauces chosen to taste and enjoy.

Nutritional Values (per serving):

Fats: 42g - Carbohydrates: 12g - Proteins: 39g - Calories: 220

2) Fondue with red shrimp, scallops and squid with rosemary mayonnaise

Preparation Time: 20 minutes

Cooking time: 5 minutes

Number of Servings: 4

Ingredients:

- 1 lb. shelled and cleaned red shrimp
- 1 lb. of cleaned scallops
- 1 lb. of cleaned squid
- 1 lemon, thinly sliced
- 6 cups fish stock
- 2 bay leaves
- Rosemary mayonnaise sauce to taste

Preparation Procedure:

Bring fish or vegetable stock to a boil over low heat in a fondue pot.

Add the lemon slices and bay leaves to the broth for flavor.

Thread the seafood with fondue forks and cook in the broth over low heat for about 5 minutes until cooked through. Dip in the rosemary mayonnaise sauce and enjoy.

Nutritional Values (per serving):

Fats: 8g - Carbohydrates: 6g - Proteins: 65g - Calories: 186

3) Chicken fondue with Asian style

Preparation Time: 25 minutes

Cooking time: 5 minutes

Number of Servings: 4

Ingredients:

- 2 lb. chicken breast, thinly sliced
- 2 cloves of garlic, finely chopped
- 1 tbsp. chopped ginger
- 6 cups chicken broth
- 2 green onions, chopped
- Soy sauce
- Barbecue sauce

Preparation Procedure:

Bring the chicken broth to a boil over low heat in a fondue pot.

Add the minced garlic, ginger, and green onion to the broth.

Stab the chicken with fondue forks and cook it in the boiling broth until fully cooked for about 5 minutes. Dip in soy sauce and barbecue sauce, and enjoy.

Nutritional Values (per serving):

Fats: 16 - Carbohydrates: 8g - Proteins: 48g - Calories: 165

4) Fondue with mixed mushrooms and soy sauce

Preparation Time: 28 minutes

Cooking time: 5 – 10 minutes

Number of Servings: 4

Ingredients:

- 2 lb. assorted mushrooms
- 2 cloves of garlic, minced
- 6 cups vegetable broth
- 1/2 cup dry white wine
- Fresh thyme leaves to taste
- Soy sauce to taste

Preparation Procedure:

Combine vegetable broth, minced garlic, thyme, and white wine in a fondue pot. Bring to a boil over low heat.

Thread the mushrooms with fondue forks and cook them in the broth over low heat for 5–10 minutes. Dip in the soy sauce and enjoy.

Nutritional Values (per serving):

Fats: 6g - Carbohydrates: 12g - Proteins: 48g - Calories: 96

5) Spicy pork and vegetable fondue

Preparation Time: 35 minutes

Cooking time: 5 – 8 minutes

Number of Servings: 4

Ingredients:

- 2 lb. pork made into thin slices
- 1/2 lb. of tofu
- 1/2 lb. mixed mushrooms
- 6 cups of spicy hot pot broth
- 1/2 lb. of leafy greens
- Soy sauce to taste
- Chili sauce to taste

Preparation Procedure:

Bring the hot broth to a boil over low heat in a fondue pot.

Arrange the assorted fondue ingredients on plates.

Stab the pork and other ingredients to taste with fondue forks and dip them into the boiling broth for about 5 to 8 minutes until cooked through. Dip them in the sauces to taste, and enjoy.

Nutritional Values (per serving):

Fats: 39g - Carbohydrates: 6g - Proteins: 34g - Calories: 249

6) Fondue with chicken, tomato and basil

Preparation Time: 32 minutes

Cooking time: 4 – 8 minutes

Number of Servings: 4

Ingredients:

- 2 lb. boneless chicken thighs, cut into small pieces
- 2 cans of diced tomatoes
- 1/2 cup fresh basil leaves

- 6 cups chicken broth
- Sauce to taste between soy sauce, garlic mayonnaise, paprika mayonnaise, barbecue sauce

Preparation Procedure:

In a fondue pot, combine chicken broth and diced tomatoes. Bring to a boil over low heat.

Add the torn basil leaves for flavor.

Using fondue forks, thread the chicken through and cook in the boiling broth until fully cooked, 4–8 minutes. Dip in the chosen sauce and enjoy.

Nutritional Values (per serving):

Fats: 9g - Carbohydrates: 5g - Proteins: 118g - Calories: 96

7) Coconut milk fondue with shrimp and mixed vegetables

Preparation Time: 34 minutes

Cooking time: 5 – 8 minutes

Number of Servings: 4

Ingredients:

- 2 lb. shrimp, shelled and cleaned
- 2 tbsp. red curry paste
- 6 cups coconut milk
- Fresh cilantro and lime wedges
- 1 lb. assorted vegetables (peppers, corn, bamboo shoots)

Preparation Procedure:

In a fondue pot, heat the coconut milk over medium heat.

Stir in the Thai red curry pastes and allow the flavors to meld. Bring to a boil over low heat.

Thread the shrimp and vegetables into fondue forks and cook in the coconut curry broth over low heat for 5-8 minutes. Garnish with fresh cilantro, and serve with lime wedges.

Nutritional Values (per serving):

Fats: 12g - Carbohydrates: 11g - Proteins: 96g - Calories: 190

8) Vegan fondue of tofu and mixed vegetables

Preparation Time: 28 minutes

Cooking time: 6 minutes

Number of Servings: 4

Ingredients:

- 2 lb. tofu, cut into cubes
- 1 lb. assorted vegetables (broccoli, carrots, peppers)
- cut into small pieces
- 6 cups vegetable broth
- Soy sauce or tamari to taste

Preparation Procedure:

Bring vegetable broth to a boil over low heat in a fondue pot.

Using fondue forks, poke in the tofu cubes and vegetables and cook in the broth over low heat for about 6 minutes until the vegetables are tender. Dip in soy sauce or tamari and enjoy.

Nutritional Values (per serving):

Fats: 12g - Carbohydrates: 9g - Proteins: 76g - Calories: 189

9) Mexican style beef fondue and jalapenos

Preparation Time: 36 minutes

Cooking time: 6 – 9 minutes

Number of Servings: 4

Ingredients:

- 1 lb. sirloin of beef, sliced
- 1 tbsp. chili powder
- 1 tsp. cumin
- 6 cups beef stock
- 1 lb. sliced jalapeños and shredded cheddar cheese
- 1 tsp. turmeric

Preparation Procedure:

Combine beef broth, chili powder, cumin, and turmeric in a fondue pot. Bring to a boil over low heat.

Thread the thinly sliced beef with fondue forks and cook in the broth over low heat for 6 to 9 minutes. Taste with sliced jalapeños and shredded cheddar cheese.

Nutritional Values (per serving):

Fats: 48g - Carbohydrates: 6g - Proteins: 118g - Calories: 246

10) Fondue of dill-flavored seafood

Preparation Time: 32 minutes

Cooking time: 5 – 8 minutes

Number of Servings: 4

Ingredients:

- 2 lb. mixed seafood (shrimp, scallops, mussels)
- 1 bunch of fresh dill for garnish
- 2 cloves of garlic
- 6 cups fish stock
- Sauces to taste such as soy sauce, paprika mayonnaise, barbecue sauce or others of your choice

Preparation Procedure:

In a fondue pot, bring the fish stock to a boil over low heat, adding the garlic and dill to the store for flavor.

Thread the mixed seafood into the fondue forks and cook in the broth over low heat for 5 to 8 minutes. Dip in the sauces to taste, and enjoy.

Nutritional Values (per serving):

Fats: 18g - Carbohydrates: 7g - Proteins: 120g - Calories: 163

11) Japanese-style beef sukiyaki fondue

Preparation Time: 32 minutes

Cooking time: 8 – 10 minutes

Number of Servings: 4

Ingredients:

- 2 lb. thinly sliced beef (ribeye)
- 1/2 cup soy sauce
- 1 lb. assorted vegetables (shiitake mushrooms, napa cabbage, tofu)
- 6 cups dashi broth or beef stock
- Udon noodles to serve

Preparation Procedure:

In a fondue pot, combine the dashi broth and soy sauce and bring to a boil over low heat.

Using fondue forks, thread the thinly sliced beef and vegetables and cook in the broth on low heat for 8 to 10 minutes until the beef is cooked and the vegetables are tender.

Serve with boiled noodles.

Nutritional Values (per serving):

Fats: 19g - Carbohydrates: 9g - Proteins: 123g - Calories: 186

12) French Beef Fondue Bourguignon Classic

Preparation Time: 42 minutes

Cooking time: 8- 10 minutes

Number of Servings: 4

Ingredients:

- 2 lb. beef tenderloin, cut into cubes
- 1/2 cup dry red wine
- 6 cups sodium-free beef broth
- Sliced mushrooms and spring onions for garnish

14) Thyme-flavored vegetarian fondue

Preparation Time: 25 minutes

Cooking time: 8 - 12 minutes

Number of Servings: 4

Ingredients:

- 6 cups vegetable broth
- 1 bunch of thyme
- 1 lb. cubes of tofu
- Cooked rice or pasta to serve
- 2 lb. assorted vegetables (carrots, broccoli, peppers, zucchini) chopped into small pieces

Preparation Procedure:

In a fondue pot, combine the thyme and vegetable broth and bring to a boil.

Using fondue forks, thread the assorted vegetables and tofu cubes and cook in the broth on low heat for about 8–12 minutes. Serve with cooked rice or noodles, and enjoy.

Nutritional Values (per serving):

Fats: 16g - Carbohydrates: 8g - Proteins: 68g - Calories: 158

15) Thai-style chicken fondue

Preparation Time: 34 minutes

Cooking time: 5 – 10 minutes

Number of Servings: 4

Ingredients:

- 2 lb. chicken breast, thinly sliced
- 2 tbsp. red curry paste
- 1 can of coconut milk
- 6 cups chicken broth
- Chopped fresh cilantro and lime wedges for garnish

Preparation Procedure:

In a fondue pot, slowly boil the chicken broth and coconut milk. Season the broth with the red curry paste and stir.

Stick in the chicken slices using fondue forks and cook in the broth on low heat for about 5 – 10 minutes. Garnish with fresh cilantro, serve with lime wedges, and enjoy.

Nutritional Values (per serving):

Fats: 19g - Carbohydrates: 7g - Proteins: 48g - Calories: 226

16) Asian-style pork fondue

Preparation Time: 35 minutes

Cooking time: 5 - 10 minutes

Number of Portions: 4

Ingredients:

- 6 cups of vegetable broth
- 2 lb. pork cheek chopped into small pieces
- 1 lb. mixed vegetables (carrots, celery, zucchini, beans) cleaned and cut into pieces
- 1 lb. bamboo cleaned and sliced

Preparation Procedure:

In a fondue pot, bring vegetable broth to a slow boil.

Using fondue forks, skewer the pork, mixed vegetables, and bamboo and cook in the simmering broth for about 5–10 minutes until cooked through. Enjoy.

Nutritional Values (per serving):

Fats: 16g - Carbohydrates: 9g - Proteins: 38g - Calories: 175

17) Korean-style beef fondue

Preparation Time: 25 minutes

Cooking time: 5 - 8 minutes

Number of Servings: 4

Ingredients:

- 2 lb. thinly sliced beef
- 6 cups of beef broth
- 1 bunch of fresh cilantros
- 1 tbsp. gochujang (Korean red bell pepper paste)
- Sliced green onions and sesame seeds for garnish

Preparation Procedure:

In a fondue pot, bring beef broth to a slow boil. Season the broth with gochujang and cilantro.

Thread the thinly sliced beef with fondue forks and cook in the broth on low heat for 5–8 minutes.

Garnish with sliced green onions and sesame seeds, and enjoy.

Nutritional Values (per serving):

Fats: 19g - Carbohydrates: 9g - Proteins: 68g - Calories: 196

18) Spicy fondue with Mexican-style chicken

Preparation Time: 36 minutes

Cooking time: 4 - 6 minutes

Number of Servings: 4

Ingredients:

- 2 lb. chicken thighs, diced
- 1 tbsp. spicy chili
- 6 cups chicken broth
- Chopped fresh cilantro, sliced radishes and lime wedges for garnish

Preparation Procedure:

Bring the chicken broth to a slow boil in a fondue pot, add the chili, and stir.

Using fondue forks, skewer the chicken and cook for about 4–6 minutes until the chicken is cooked. Garnish with chopped fresh cilantro, sliced radishes, and lime wedges.

Nutritional Values (per serving):

Fats: 19g - Carbohydrates: 22g - Proteins: 56g - Calories: 224

19) Sea bass fondue

Preparation Time: 28 minutes

Cooking time: 1 – 4 minutes

Number of Servings: 4

Ingredients:

- 6 cups of fish stock
- 1 green onion
- 1 bunch of fresh parsley
- 2 lb. filleted, cleaned and chopped sea bass
- Garlic butter for dipping
- Mayonnaise sauce

Preparation Procedure:

In a fondue pot, bring the fish stock to a boil. Add the onion and parsley to the broth.

Stick in the fish pieces using fondue forks and cook in the broth on low heat for about 1–4 minutes.

Dip in garlic butter and mayonnaise, and enjoy.

Nutritional Values (per serving):

Fats: 12g - Carbohydrates: 9g - Proteins: 78g - Calories: 184

20) Japanese classic Sukiyaki fondue

Preparation Time: 33 minutes

Cooking Time: 2 - 4 minutes

Number of Servings: 4

Ingredients:

- 6 cups dashi broth or beef broth
- 1 lb. cabbage, tofu and shiitake mushrooms
- Sukiyaki sauce to taste
- Cooked udon noodles to serve
- 2 lb. thinly sliced beef

Preparation Procedure:

Bring the dashi or beef stock to a slow boil in a fondue pot.

Using fondue forks, skewer the thinly sliced beef, Napa cabbage, tofu, and shiitake mushrooms and cook in the simmering broth for about 2–4 minutes over low heat. Accompany with cooked noodles, dip in the sauce, and enjoy.

Nutritional Values (per serving):

Fats: 19g - Carbohydrates: 11g - Proteins: 89g - Calories: 239

21) Classic Chinoise fondue

Preparation Time: 34 minutes

Cooking Time: 5 - 8 minutes

Number of Servings: 4

Ingredients:

- 2 lb. beef cut into carpaccio
- 2 tsp. Worcestershire sauce
- 6/8 cups beef stock
- 2 oz. dried Chinese mushrooms
- 5-6 drops of tabasco sauce
- 1 glass of dry red wine
- Roquefort sauce to taste
- Lemon sauce to taste
- Garlic sauce to taste
- Mustard sauce to taste

Preparation Procedure:

Take a bowl with water and pour in the mushrooms so that they are revived.

Then get the fondue pot, pour in the broth, Tabasco, wine, revived mushrooms, and Worcestershire sauce, and stir everything together.

Warm over low heat until it comes to a slow boil. Using fondue forks, pierce the veal and cook for about 5 to 8 minutes.

Dip the cooked meat into the various sauces and enjoy.

Nutritional Values (per serving):

Fats: 26g - Carbohydrates: 8g - Proteins: 76g - Calories: 215

22) Fondue Shabu Shabu

Preparation Time: 28 minutes

Cooking Time: 2 - 4 minutes

Number of Servings: 4

Ingredients:

- 1 lb. thin slices of beef
- 8 oz. shredded tofu
- 8 oz. shredded escarole
- 4 oz. of soybean sprouts
- 10 chopped mushrooms
- 2 chopped spring onions
- 1 carrot shredded
- 6/8 cups beef stock

Preparation Procedure:

Take the fondue pot, pour in the beef broth, and bring to a boil.

Pour the vegetables, mushrooms, and tofu into the broth and cook until the vegetables are crispy and the tofu is soft.

Using fondue forks, pierce the meat and cook it in the broth for 2 to 4 minutes until cooked.

Nutritional Values (per serving):

Fats: 56g - Carbohydrates: 4g - Proteins: 79g - Calories: 238

Chapter 7: Chocolate fondue recipes

1) Milk chocolate fondue

Preparation time: 20 minutes

Cooking time: 15 minutes

Number of servings: 4

Ingredients:

- 14 ounces milk chocolate
- 1 cup fresh liquid cream
- 1 tablespoon walnut liqueur
- 2 teaspoons vanilla extract
- 1 teaspoon almonds

Dippers: Sliced banana, Strawberries, Marshmallows

Preparation procedure:

Pour the cream into a fondue pan and cook for a few minutes just until it boils.

Add the chocolate, the walnut liqueur, and the vanilla extract, and cook over low heat for 15 minutes until it becomes a smooth mixture. Add the almonds and mix with a wooden spoon.

Leave the pot to warm on a fondue burner, and immerse the banana slices, strawberries, and marshmallows.

Nutritional values (per serving):

Fat: 16 g - Carbohydrates: 21 g - Protein: 5g - Calories: 455

2) Dark chocolate and mint fondue

Preparation time: 30 minutes

Cooking time: 15-25 minutes

Number of servings: 6

Preparation Procedure:

Combine the beef stock and red wine in a fondue pot and bring to a slow boil.

Stick in the beef cubes using fondue forks and cook in the broth on low heat for about 8–10 minutes. Garnish with sliced, cooked mushrooms and fresh spring onions.

Nutritional Values (per serving):

Fats: 19g - Carbohydrates: 9g - Proteins: 38g - Calories: 174

13) Moroccan-style lamb and chickpea fondue

Preparation Time: 40 minutes

Cooking time: 8 - 12 minutes

Number of Servings: 4

Ingredients:

- 2 lb. of stewed lamb, cut into cubes
- 1 tbsp. ground cumin
- 1 tbsp. ground coriander
- 1 tbsp. ground cinnamon
- 6 cups lamb or vegetable stock
- 1 can of chickpeas, drained and rinsed
- Chopped fresh coriander for garnish

Preparation Procedure:

Bring lamb or vegetable stock to a slow boil in a fondue pot. Season the lamb cubes with cumin, coriander, and cinnamon.

Using fondue forks, thread the lamb cubes and chickpeas through and cook in the broth on low heat for about 8–12 minutes, until the lamb is tender.

Garnish with fresh chopped cilantro, and enjoy.

Nutritional Values (per serving):

Fats: 18g - Carbohydrates: 9g - Proteins: 47g - Calories: 178

Ingredients:

- 14 ounces dark chocolate crumbles
- 1 cup fresh heavy cream
- 1 tablespoon aromatic liquor
- 1 teaspoon mint extract
- 1/2 teaspoon coriander extract

Dippers: Strawberries, Chocolate brownie

Preparation procedure:

In a fondue pot, pour the aromatic liquor and fresh cream and cook for 5 minutes, until simmering.

Add dark chocolate, mint, and coriander, and cook for 15-20 minutes until smooth.

Heat the pan on a fondue burner and immerse the strawberries and chocolate brownie.

Nutritional values (per serving):

Fat: 16 g - Carbohydrates: 22 g - Protein: 4.5g - Calories: 385

3) White chocolate and blackberry fondue

Preparation time: 20 minutes

Cooking time: 15 minutes

Number of servings: 4

Ingredients:

- 10 ounces chopped white chocolate
- 1 cup fresh heavy cream
- 1/2 cup blackberries
- 1 tablespoon of berry liqueur

Dippers: Pieces of Angel cake, Sliced banana

Preparation procedure:

In a fondue pot, pour the liquid cream and cook for a few minutes just until it simmers.

Add the chopped white chocolate and the berry liqueur, and cook over low heat for 15 minutes until a homogeneous mixture is created. Add the blackberries to the chocolate fondue and mix well.

Place the hot pan on the fondue stove and immerse the angel cake and banana slices.

Nutritional Values (per serving):

Fats: 21g - Carbohydrates: 18g - Proteins: 3,5g - Calories: 370

4) Dark chocolate and orange fondue

Preparation time: 25 minutes

Cooking time: 15-20 minutes

Number of servings: 4

Ingredients:

- 1 orange peel
- 12 ounces dark chocolate, chopped
- 1 cup fresh heavy cream
- 1 tablespoon aromatic liquor
- Dippers:
- Orange slices
- Cherries
- Biscuits

Preparation procedure:

Take a fondue pot, pour in the fresh cream and aromatic liquor, and cook for a few minutes until it boils.

Add the dark chocolate and orange zest and cook for 20 minutes, stirring frequently, until a smooth mixture is created. Place the hot pot on a fondue burner, and immerse the orange slices, cherries, and dry biscuits.

Nutritional values (per serving):

Fat: 19.5 g - Carbohydrates: 24 g - Protein: 4.8g - Calories: 315

4) Milk chocolate and peanut butter fondue

Preparation time: 20 minutes

Cooking time: 15 minutes

Number of servings: 6

Ingredients:

- 14 ounces milk chocolate, chopped
- 1 cup fresh heavy cream
- 1/2 cup creamy peanut butter
- 1 tablespoon vanilla extract

Dippers: Banana slices, Marshmallows, Pretzel slices

Preparation procedure:

In a fondue pot, pour the fresh liquid cream into the vanilla extract and simmer for a few minutes.

Add the milk chocolate and peanut butter and simmer for 15 minutes, until smooth.

Leave the pot hot on the fondue stove and immerse the banana, marshmallows, and pretzel slices.

Nutritional values (per serving):

Fat: 17 g - Carbohydrates: 24g - Protein: 4g - Calories: 260

6) Dark chocolate and salted caramel fondue

Preparation time: 30 minutes

Cooking time: 20-25 minutes

Number of servings: 6

Ingredients:

- 14 ounces dark chocolate, chopped
- 1 cup fresh heavy cream
- 1/2 cup salted caramel sauce
- 1 tablespoon acacia honey
- 1 tablespoon vanilla extract

Dippers: Apple slices, Brownie cake pieces

Preparation procedure:

In a fondue pot, pour the fresh cream vanilla extract and heat for a few minutes until it boils.

Add dark chocolate and stir well for 15-20 minutes until the fondue is smooth.

In a separate small pot, pour the salted caramel sauce and heat it for a few minutes. Transfer the sauce to the fondue and mix well. Put the pan on hot and immerse the apple slices and the brownie cake.

Nutritional values (per serving):

Fat: 21.5 g - Carbohydrates: 24 g - Protein: 4.8g - Calories: 350

7) White chocolate and pistachio fondue

Preparation time: 25 minutes

Cooking time: 15-20 minutes

Number of servings: 4

Ingredients:

- 10 ounces of chopped white chocolate
- 1 cup fresh heavy cream
- 1 tablespoon aromatic liquor
- 1 tablespoon chopped pistachios

Dippers: Chocolate cookies, Strawberries, Marshmallows

Preparation procedure:

Pour the fresh cream and aromatic liquor in a fondue pot, and cook for a few minutes until it boils.

Add the white chocolate-chopped pistachios and cook over low heat for 15-20 minutes until a smooth mixture is obtained.

Place the hot pot on a fondue burner, and dip the chocolate biscuits, strawberries, and marshmallows.

Nutritional values (per serving):

Fat: 21 g - Carbohydrates: 22 g - Protein: 3.6g - Calories: 300

8) Dark chocolate and coffee fondue

Preparation time: 20 minutes

Cooking time: 15 minutes

Number of servings: 4

Ingredients:

- 10 ounces dark chocolate, chopped
- 1 cup fresh heavy cream
- 1 tablespoon of coffee granules
- 1 teaspoon of ground coffee

Dippers: Cookies, Strawberries

Preparation procedure:

In a fondue pan, pour the liquid cream and heat for a few minutes until it simmers.

Add the dark chocolate, the coffee powder, and the coffee granules, and cook for 15 minutes until you obtain a uniform mixture.

Leave the pan on a fondue burner, and immerse the biscuits and strawberries.

Nutritional values (per serving):

Fat: 15 g - Carbohydrates: 21g - Protein: 4.5g - Calories: 312

9) Milk chocolate and hazelnut fondue

Preparation time: 25 minutes

Cooking time: 20 minutes

Number of servings: 6

Ingredients:

- 12 milk chocolate, chopped
- 1 cup fresh heavy cream
- 1/2 cup hazelnut cream
- 1 tablespoon toasted hazelnuts
- 1 tablespoon aromatic liquor

Dippers: Sliced bananas, Pound cake cubes, Strawberries

Preparation procedure:

Take a fondue pot, pour the liquid cream aromatic liquor, and cook for a few minutes until it simmers.

Add the milk chocolate hazelnuts, and cook for 20 minutes until you obtain a smooth mixture.

Heat the pot on a fondue burner, and immerse the banana slices, pound cake cubes, and strawberries.

Nutritional values (per serving):

Fat: 16.5 g - Carbohydrates: 21 g - Protein: 4g - Calories: 410

10) Dark chocolate and cinnamon fondue

Preparation time: 30 minutes

Cooking time: 20-25 minutes

Number of servings: 4

Ingredients:

- 10 ounces dark chocolate crumbles
- 1 cup fresh heavy cream
- 2 tablespoons aromatic liquor
- 1 tablespoon ground cinnamon

Dippers: Churros, Banana slices, Pineapple pieces

Preparation procedure:

In a fondue pot, pour the liquid cream into the aromatic liquor and heat for a few minutes until it simmers.

Add the dark chocolate and the cinnamon powder, and cook for 20-25 minutes until the mixture is smooth.

Place the hot pan on a fondue stove, and immerse the churros, pineapple pieces, and banana slices.

Nutritional values (per serving):

Fat: 15.5 g - Carbohydrates: 22 g - Protein: 4.2g - Calories: 375

11) Milk chocolate and coconut fondue

Preparation time: 20 minutes

Cooking time: 15 minutes

Number of servings: 4

Ingredients:

- 10 ounces milk chocolate, crumbled
- 1 cup fresh heavy cream
- 1/2 cup shredded coconut
- 1 tablespoon brown sugar
- 1 tablespoon vanilla extract

Dippers: Strawberries, Marshmallow

Preparation procedure:

Pour the cream, vanilla extract, and brown sugar into a fondue pot and cook for a few minutes until it begins to simmer.

Add the milk chocolate and the grated coconut, and cook for 15 minutes until the mixture is well combined.

Leave the pan to warm on the fondue stove and dip the marshmallows and strawberries.

Nutritional values (per serving):

Fat: 20 g - Carbohydrates: 24 g - Protein: 3.8g - Calories: 320

12) Fondue with chocolate, mint and rosemary

Preparation time: 25 minutes

Cooking time: 15-20 minutes

Number of servings: 6

Ingredients:

- 14 ounces dark chocolate, chopped
- 1 cup fresh heavy cream
- 1 tablespoon whole milk

- 1 teaspoon fresh mint extract
- 1 teaspoon of rosemary

Dippers: Biscuits, Strawberries, Mint chocolates

Preparation procedure:

In a fondue pot, pour the liquid cream and the milk and cook for a few minutes just until it boils.

Add the dark chocolate, mint extract, and rosemary, and cook for 15-20 minutes until you obtain a smooth mixture.

Leave the pan to heat on a fondue burner, and dip in dry biscuits, strawberries, and mint chocolates.

Nutritional values (per serving):

Fat: 18.5 g - Carbohydrates: 22 g - Protein: 4.2g - Calories: 360

13) Chocolate, pine nut and butter fondue

Preparation time: 25 minutes

Cooking time: 20 minutes

Number of servings: 4

Ingredients:

- 12 ounces chopped dark chocolate
- 1 cup fresh heavy cream
- 1/2 cup pine nuts
- 1 tablespoon salted butter

Dippers: Apple slices, Biscuits

Preparation procedure:

In a fondue pot, pour the liquid cream and the salted butter, and heat for a few minutes over low heat.

Add the dark chocolate and the pine nuts, and cook for 20 minutes, stirring frequently to obtain a thick mixture.

Leave the pot to heat on the fondue stove, and dip the dry biscuits and apple slices.

Nutritional values (per serving):

Fat: 17.5 g - Carbohydrates: 24 g - Protein: 4.2g - Calories: 325

14) Dark chocolate and melon fondue

Preparation time: 30 minutes

Cooking time: 15-20 minutes

Number of servings: 6

Ingredients:

- 1 melon cut into cubes
- 14 ounces dark chocolate crumbles
- 1 cup fresh heavy cream
- 1 tablespoon aromatic liquor

Dippers: Diced melon, Biscuits

Preparation procedure:

Pour the liquid cream and aromatic liquor into a fondue pot and heat until it simmers.

Gently add the dark chocolate and cook, stirring often, for 15-20 minutes, until the mixture is smooth. Add half of the diced melon and mix for a few minutes.

Leave the pot hot on the fondue stove, and immerse the other half of the diced melon.

Nutritional values (per serving):

Fat: 19 g - Carbohydrates: 24 g - Protein: 4.5g - Calories: 350

15) Semi-sweet chocolate and almond fondue

Preparation time: 25 minutes

Cooking time: 20 minutes

Number of servings: 4

Ingredients:

- 10 ounces semisweet chocolate, chopped
- 1 cup fresh heavy cream
- 1/2 cup almonds
- 1 tablespoon brown sugar

Dippers: Banana slices, Chocolate cookies, Marshmallows

Preparation procedure:

Pour the liquid cream and brown sugar into a fondue pot and heat until it boils.

Add the chopped semisweet chocolate almonds and simmer for 20 minutes, until thick.

Leave the pot on the fondue stove, and dip the banana slices, chocolate biscuits, and marshmallows.

Nutritional values (per serving):

Fat: 16.5 g - Carbohydrates: 22 g - Protein: 4.1g - Calories: 318

16) Milk chocolate and barley fondue

Preparation time: 25 minutes

Cooking time: 20 minutes

Number of servings: 4

Ingredients:

- 12 ounces milk chocolate crumbles
- 1 cup fresh heavy cream
- 1 tablespoon cocoa powder
- 1 teaspoon granulated sugar

Dippers: Pound cake cubes, Banana slices

Preparation procedure:

Pour the fresh liquid cream and granulated sugar into a fondue pot and heat until it simmer.

Add the milk chocolate to the barley powder and cook over low heat for 20 minutes, stirring frequently to obtain a homogeneous mixture.

Place the hot pot on the fondue stove, and dip the pound cake cubes and banana slices.

Nutritional values (per serving):

Fat: 14.5 g - Carbohydrates: 16 g - Protein: 3.8g - Calories: 318

17) White chocolate fondue, strawberries and berries

Preparation time: 20 minutes

Cooking time: 15 minutes

Number of servings: 6

Ingredients:

- 14 ounces white chocolate, broken into cubes
- 1 cup fresh heavy cream
- 1 cup sliced strawberries
- 2 tablespoons of berries

Dippers: Mini donuts, Chocolate cookies, 1 cup of Strawberry slices

Preparation procedure:

Take a fondue pot and pour in the liquid cream; heat for a few minutes until simmering.

Add the white chocolate, 1/2 cup sliced strawberries, and the berries, and cook for 15 minutes until well combined.

Leave the pot on the fondue stove, and immerse the mini donuts, chocolate chip cookies, and the other 1/2 cup of strawberry slices.

Nutritional values (per serving):

Fat: 16.5 g - Carbohydrates: 18 g - Protein: 4.5g - Calories: 305

18) Dark chocolate and gooseberry fondue

Preparation time: 20 minutes

Cooking time: 15 minutes

Number of servings: 4

Ingredients:

- 12 ounces chopped dark chocolate
- 1 cup fresh heavy cream
- 1/2 cup gooseberries
- 1 tablespoon blueberry liqueur

Dippers: Marshmallow, Biscuits

Preparation procedure:

Pour the liquid cream and the blueberry liqueur into a fondue pot and heat for a few minutes.

Add the dark chocolate to the gooseberries, and cook, stirring often, for 15 minutes, until the mixture is smooth.

Leave the pan to heat on a fondue burner, and immerse the dry biscuits and marshmallows.

Nutritional values (per serving):

Fat: 20 g - Carbohydrates: 21.5 g - Protein: 4.8g - Calories: 365

19) Dark chocolate, cocoa and kiwi fondue

Preparation time: 25 minutes

Cooking time: 20 minutes

Number of servings: 6

Ingredients:

- 12 ounces dark chocolate, chopped
- 1 cup fresh heavy cream
- 1 cup sliced kiwis
- 1 tablespoon cocoa powder
- 1 tablespoon of aromatic liqueur

Dippers: Chocolate cake cubes, Strawberries

Preparation procedure:

Pour the liquid cream and aromatic liqueur into a fondue pot and heat until it boils.

Add the dark chocolate and cocoa powder and cook for 20 minutes, until the mixture is well blended. Add 1 cup of sliced kiwi and mix for a few minutes.

Leave the pan on the fondue stove, and immerse the chocolate cake cubes and strawberries.

Nutritional values (per serving):

Fat: 18.5 g - Carbohydrates: 22 g - Protein: 3.6g - Calories: 365

20) White chocolate, cinnamon and ginger fondue

Preparation time: 20 minutes

Cooking time: 15 minutes

Number of servings: 4

Ingredients:

- 10 ounces white chocolate, finely chopped
- 1/2 cup fresh heavy cream
- 1 tablespoon of aromatic liqueur
- 1 teaspoon ground cinnamon
- 1 teaspoon powdered ginger

Dippers: Banana slices, pretzel

Preparation procedure:

Pour the liquid cream and aromatic liqueur into a fondue pot and heat until it simmers.

Add the white chocolate, ginger, and cinnamon, and cook over medium heat for 15 minutes until the mixture becomes thick.

Leave the pan warm on a fondue burner, and immerse the banana slices and pretzels.

Nutritional values (per serving):

Fat: 15 g - Carbohydrates: 22.5 g - Protein: 4.4g - Calories: 380

21) Semi-sweet chocolate fondue with tangerine

Preparation time: 25 minutes

Cooking time: 20 minutes

Number of servings: 4

Ingredients:

- 1 tangerine peel
- 12 ounces semi-sweet chocolate
- 1 cup fresh heavy cream
- 1 tablespoon of aromatic liqueur

Dippers: Tangerine segments, Cookies

Preparation procedure:

Pour the fresh liquid cream and the aromatic liqueur into a fondue pot and heat for a few minutes.

Add the semi-sweet chocolate and cook for 15 minutes, until melted. Place the orange zest in the pan and cook for another 5 minutes.

Keep the pan warm on the fondue stove and immerse the tangerine segments and biscuits.

Nutritional values (per serving):

Fat: 14 g - Carbohydrates: 21g - Protein: 3.4g - Calories: 265

Chapter 8: Fondue recipes for two

1)Fondue cheese and kirsch

Preparation Time: 23 minutes

Cooking Time: 6 – 8 minutes

Number of Servings: 2

Ingredients:

- 7 oz. Swiss cheese, grated
- 1 clove of garlic, peeled
- 7 oz. Gruyere cheese, grated
- Freshly ground black pepper
- 1 cup of dry white wine
- 2 tbsp. kirsch (cherry brandy)
- 1 tbsp. lemon juice
- 1 tbsp. cornstarch

Dippers: Cubed bread

Preparation Procedure:

Scrub the inside of a fondue pot with the garlic clove for flavor. Add the white wine and lemon juice to the pot and heat slowly over low heat.

Add the grated cheese gradually, stirring constantly, until melted and smooth.

Mix the cornstarch and Kirsch in a small bowl to make a paste and cook for 6 to 8 minutes. Add it to the cheese mixture while stirring.

Season with black pepper to taste. Using fondue forks, pierce the bread cubes, dip them into the cheese fondue, and taste.

Nutritional Values (per serving):

Fats: 68g - Carbohydrates: 39g - Proteins: 48g - Calories: 340

2) Soy flavored beef fondue

Preparation Time: 26 minutes

Cooking Time: 6 – 9 minutes

Number of Servings: 2

Ingredients:

- 1 lb. beef tenderloin, cut into cubes
- 1 clove of garlic, minced
- 1 cup of beef stock without salt
- 1 tsp. vegetable oil
- 1 tbsp. soy sauce
- Dipping sauces to taste (horseradish, barbecue, garlic aioli)

Preparation Procedure:

In the fondue pot, heat the beef broth and combine it with the minced garlic, soy sauce, and vegetable oil. Bring everything to a boil over low heat.

Using fondue forks, skewer the beef and cook it in the hot broth for about 6 to 9 minutes. Dip the cooked beef in the sauces of your choice and enjoy.

Nutritional Values (per serving):

Fats: 18g - Carbohydrates: 6g - Proteins: 49g - Calories: 268

3) Fruit and chocolate fondue

Preparation Time: 23 minutes

Cooking time: few seconds

Number of Servings: 2

Ingredients:

- 7 oz. chopped dark chocolate
- 1/4 cup hazelnut cream
- 1/2 cup heavy cream

Dippers: 1 lb. fresh strawberries, sliced bananas and marshmallows for dipping

Preparation Procedure:

Get the fondue pot, pour the chopped dark chocolate, and melt it over low heat.

Add the heavy cream to the melted chocolate and stir. Stir until creamy and smooth. Add the hazelnut cream and stir.

Pierce the fruit and marshmallows with fondue forks, dip them in the resulting cream for a few seconds, and enjoy.

Nutritional Values (per serving):

Fats: 65g - Carbohydrates: 24g - Proteins: 38g - Calories: 320

4) Italian-style mozzarella and tomato fondue

Preparation Time: 18 minutes

Cooking time: 2 minutes

Number of Servings: 2

Ingredients:

- 7 oz. diced mozzarella cheese
- Fresh basil leaves
- 1/2 cup tomato sauce

Dippers: Cherry tomatoes and chunks of Italian bread

Preparation Procedure:

Warm the tomato sauce in a small saucepan. Alternate layers of mozzarella cheese cubes and fresh basil leaves are in the fondue pot.

Drizzle the hot tomato sauce over the cheese and basil and cook for 2 minutes.

Dip the cherry tomatoes and bread pieces into the tomato cheese sauce using fondue forks.

Nutritional Values (per serving):

Fats: 36g - Carbohydrates: 69g - Proteins: 19g - Calories: 365

5) Cajun spicy seafood fondue

Preparation Time: 28 minutes

Cooking time: 6 -8 minutes

Number of Servings: 2

Ingredients:

- 7 oz. shrimp, shelled and cleaned
- 1 tbsp. Cajun seasoning
- 2 cups fish stock
- 7 oz. of scallops
- Cocktail sauce for dipping

Preparation Procedure:

Warm the fish stock in a fondue pot and stir in the Cajun seasoning.

Stab the seafood with a fork and cook them in the boiling broth for 6 to 8 minutes until they are cooked. Dip them in the cocktail sauce and enjoy.

Nutritional Values (per serving):

Fats: 38g - Carbohydrates: 6g - Proteins: 69g - Calories: 239

6) Fruit fondue and chocolate hazelnut preztel

Preparation Time: 28 minutes

Cooking time: 2 minutes

Number of Servings: 2

Ingredients:

- 7 oz. Swiss milk chocolate, chopped
- 1/4 cup almond butter
- 1/2 cup heavy cream

Dippers: 1 lb. sliced bananas, apple slices and pretzels

Preparation Procedure:

In a fondue pot, melt milk chocolate and heavy cream over low heat and stir.

Mix until creamy and smooth. Add the almond butter and stir.

Pierce the fruit and pretzels with fondue forks, dip them in the resulting cream for about 2 minutes, and enjoy.

Nutritional Values (per serving):

Fats: 56g - Carbohydrates: 69g - Proteins: 96g - Calories: 380

7) Classic vegetable fondue with spinach or artichoke dip

Preparation Time: 29 minutes

Cooking time: few seconds

Number of Servings: 2

Ingredients:

- 7 oz. cubed mozzarella cheese
- 1/2 cup spinach or artichoke dip

Dippers: Slices of baguette and raw vegetables (tomatoes, carrots, celery, onions)

Preparation Procedure:

Alternate layers of mozzarella cheese cubes and spoonsful of spinach or artichoke sauce in a fondue pot. Warm over low heat until mozzarella cheese is melted.

Use fondue forks to dip baguette slices and raw vegetables into this creamy sauce for a few seconds and enjoy.

Nutritional Values (per serving):

Fats: 25g - Carbohydrates: 89g - Proteins: 38g - Calories: 248

8) Fruit caramel fondue and preztel

Preparation Time: 19 minutes

Cooking time: few seconds

Number of Servings: 2

Ingredients:

- 7 oz. of caramel squares
- 1/4 cup heavy cream

Dippers: Pretzels, apple slices and marshmallows for dipping

Preparation Procedure:

In the fondue pot, melt the caramel squares over low heat and add the heavy cream, stirring.

Mix until smooth and creamy. Pierce the pretzel sticks, apple slices, and marshmallows with fondue forks, dip them for a few seconds in the fondue, and enjoy.

Nutritional Values (per serving):

Fats: 65g - Carbohydrates: 56g - Proteins: 23g - Calories: 329

9) Cheese fondue with vegetables and baguette

Preparation Time: 32 minutes

Cooking time: 2 – 3 minutes

Number of Servings: 2

Ingredients:

- 7 oz. Gruyere cheese, grated
- 1 cup of dry white wine
- 7 oz. Emmental cheese, grated
- 1 tbsp. lemon juice
- 1 clove of garlic, divided in half
- 1 tbsp. cornstarch
- Freshly ground black pepper

Dippers: Cubed French bread and blanched mixed vegetables (carrots, celery, tomatoes, fennel)

Preparation Procedure:

Scrub the inside of a fondue pot with a garlic clove cut in half. In a separate bowl, mix the grated cheese with the cornstarch.

Add the wine and lemon juice to the fondue pot and heat gently over low heat for 2-3 minutes.

Add the cheese mixture gradually, stirring until smooth and creamy. Season with black pepper. Using fondue forks, pierce the bread and vegetables, dip into the cheese fondue, and enjoy.

Nutritional Values (per serving):

Fats: 89g - Carbohydrates: 56g - Proteins: 38g - Calories: 340

10) Cheese fondue with mushrooms and truffle

Preparation Time: 31 minutes

Cooking Time: 5 – 7 minutes

Number of Servings: 2

Ingredients:

- 7 oz. Gruyere cheese, grated
- 7 oz. sliced mixed mushrooms (shiitake, cremini, etc.)
- 1 clove of garlic, minced
- 1 glass of dry white wine
- 1 tbsp. truffle oil

Dippers: Diced crusty bread and steamed asparagus

Preparation Procedure:

In a fondue pot, heat the minced garlic and dry white wine. Add grated Gruyere cheese gradually, stirring until melted and smooth.

In a separate pan, sauté mixed mushrooms in truffle oil until tender. Transfer the mushrooms to the fondue pot and stir. Cook for 5 to 7 minutes. Pierce and dip the diced crusty bread and steamed asparagus using fondue forks, and enjoy.

Nutritional Values (per serving):

Fats: 59g - Carbohydrates: 46g - Proteins: 89g - Calories: 376

11) Fondue with Emmental and hummus

Preparation time: 30 minutes

Cooking time: 25 minutes

Number of servings: 2

Ingredients:

- 8 ounces of Emmental cheese
- 1/2 cup hummus
- 2 tablespoons dry white wine
- 2 tablespoons extra virgin olive oil
- 1 tablespoon lemon juice
- 1 teaspoon coriander powder

Dippers: Carrots, Cucumber slices, Roasted bread cubes

Preparation procedure:

Pour the white wine, olive oil, and lemon juice in a fondue pot, and heat for 5 minutes.

Add the Emmental cheese, and cook over low heat for 15 minutes, until the mixture is compact; gently pour the hummus into the pan, and cook for about 5 minutes.

Keep the pot warm on a fondue burner, and serve with baby carrots, cucumber slices, and cubes of roasted bread.

Nutritional values (per serving):

Fat: 27 g - Carbohydrates: 11.5 g - Protein: 4.6 g - Calories: 350

12) Goat cheese and apricot fondue

Preparation time: 25 minutes

Cooking time: 20 minutes

Number of servings: 2

Ingredients:

- 8 ounces goat cheese, sliced
- 8 ounces grated Gruyere cheese

- 1 cup dry white wine
- 2 tablespoons cup of apricot jam
- 1 teaspoon ground black pepper
- 1 teaspoon of salt

Dippers: Bread baguette cut into slices, Broccoli florets, Apricots

Preparation procedure:

Take a fondue pot, pour in the white wine and the apricot jam, and heat for a few minutes.

Add the goat cheese and Gruyere cheese to the pot and cook, frequently stirring, for 20 minutes, until cheese is totally dissolved. Season with black pepper and salt.

Place the hot pot on a fondue burner, and immerse the apricots, broccoli florets, and baguette slices.

Nutritional values (per serving):

Fat: 18.5 g - Carbohydrates: 12 g - Protein: 8.4 g - Calories: 190

13) Salted ricotta and olive fondue

Preparation time: 25 minutes

Cooking time: 20 minutes

Number of servings: 2

Ingredients:

- 8 ounces of salted ricotta
- 6 ounces crumbled feta cheese
- 1/2 cup Greek yogurt
- 2 tablespoons pitted and chopped black olives
- 1 tablespoon fresh oregano
- 1 teaspoon ground black pepper

Dippers: Cucumber slices, Pieces of pita bread, Cherry tomatoes, Black olives

Preparation procedure:

Place the Greek yogurt and crumbled feta in a fondue pot and cook over low heat for 5 minutes.

Add the salted ricotta to the black olives, and cook for about 15 minutes until the cheese is melted. Sprinkle with fresh oregano and ground black pepper.

Keep the pot warm on a fondue burner, and serve with black olives, cherry tomatoes, pita bread, and cucumber slices.

Nutritional values (per serving):

Fat: 22 g - Carbohydrates: 14 g - Protein: 6.8 g - Calories: 310

14) Spicy chocolate and peanut fondue

Preparation time: 25 minutes

Cooking time: 15-20 minutes

Number of servings: 2

Ingredients:

- 1 cup dark chocolate
- 1/2 cup peanut butter
- 2 tablespoons coconut milk
- 2 tablespoons of fresh heavy cream
- 1 tablespoon chili liqueur
- 1 teaspoon chili powder

Dippers: Cinnamon cake slices, Biscuits

Preparation procedure:

Pour the peanut butter, coconut milk, fresh heavy cream, and chili liqueur into a fondue pot and heat for a few minutes until simmering.

Add the dark chocolate chili powder, and cook over low heat for 15-20 minutes until the mixture becomes thick.

Keep the pan warm on a fondue burner, and immerse the dry biscuits and slices of cinnamon cake.

Nutritional values (per serving):

Fat: 22 g - Carbohydrates: 11 g - Protein: 10.5 g - Calories: 360

15) Milk chocolate and raspberry fondue

Preparation time: 20 minutes

Cooking time: 15 minutes

Number of servings: 2

Ingredients:

- 1 cup milk chocolate
- 1/2 cup fresh heavy cream
- 2 tablespoons fresh raspberries
- 1 tablespoon herbal liqueur

Dippers: Banana slices, Strawberries, Biscuits

Preparation procedure:

Pour the liquid cream and herb liqueur into a fondue bowl and heat for a few minutes until simmering.

Add the milk chocolate and cook, stirring occasionally, for 15 minutes, until a compact mixture is created; add the fresh raspberries and mix for a few minutes.

Place the pot warm on a fondue burner, and immerse slices of bananas, strawberries, and dry biscuits.

Nutritional values (per serving):

Fat: 27 g - Carbohydrates: 16 g - Protein: 3.6g - Calories: 380

16) Cheddar and chili cheese fondue

Preparation time: 30 minutes

Cooking time: 15-20 minutes

Number of servings: 2

Ingredients:

- 1 whole clove of garlic
- 8 ounces cheddar cheese, shredded
- 8 ounces cream cheese
- 1/2 cup white wine
- 2 tablespoons of chili pepper
- 1 teaspoon black pepper

Dippers: French fries, Pretzel slices

Preparation procedure:

Take a fondue pot and rub the garlic clove evenly on the bottom; pour in the white wine and heat for a few minutes.

Add the cheddar cheese, cream cheese, and chili pepper, and cook for 15-20 minutes, until cheese is totally dissolved. Sprinkle with black pepper, and leave warm on a fondue burner.

Serve with pretzel slices and chips.

Nutritional values (per serving):

Fat: 16.5 g - Carbohydrates: 12 g - Protein: 14 g - Calories: 295

17) Dark chocolate and pineapple fondue

Preparation time: 25 minutes

Cooking time: 20 minutes

Number of servings: 2

Ingredients:

- 8 ounces chopped dark chocolate
- 1 cup fresh heavy cream
- 1/2 cup pineapple juice
- 1 tablespoon of aromatic liqueur
- 1 teaspoon granulated sugar

Dippers: Pineapple slices, Cake cubes with apricot jam

Preparation procedure:

Take a fondue pot and pour in the liquid cream, the pineapple juice, the aromatic liqueur, and heat for a few minutes until it simmers.

Add the dark chocolate, and cook, stirring often, for 20 minutes, until the mixture becomes thick. Sprinkle the granulated sugar over the top, and leave the pot on a fondue burner.

Serve with pineapple slices and cake cubes with apricot jam.

Nutritional values (per serving):

Fat: 22.5 g - Carbohydrates: 19 g - Protein: 4.1g - Calories: 325

18) Cream cheese and artichoke fondue

Preparation time: 30 minutes

Cooking time: 25 minutes

Number of servings: 2

Ingredients:

- 1 whole clove of garlic
- 8 ounces cream cheese
- 8 ounces grated Parmesan cheese
- 1/2 cup dry white wine
- 1/2 cup cooked and chopped artichokes

Dippers: Carrots, Slices of baguette bread, French fries

Preparation procedure:

Take a fondue pot and sprinkle the whole garlic over the bottom; add the white wine and simmer for a few minutes.

Add the grated parmesan and cream cheese in that order, and cook for 20 minutes, until cheese is totally dissolved; add the cooked artichokes and cook over low heat for 5 minutes.

Keep the pot warm on a fondue burner, and immerse the french fries, baby carrots, and slices of baguette bread.

Nutritional values (per serving):

Fat: 19.5 g - Carbohydrates: 14 g - Protein: 8.5 g - Calories: 340

19) Mixed cheese and red onion fondue

Preparation time: 30 minutes

Cooking time: 25 minutes

Number of servings: 2

Ingredients:

- 1 red onion diced
- 8 ounces Emmental cheese

- 8 ounces goat cheese
- 8 ounces cheddar cheese
- 1/2 cup white wine
- 1 tablespoon chili powder
- 2 teaspoons black pepper

Dippers: Strips of red pepper, Strips of chicken, Crunchy bread cubes

Preparation procedure:

Pour the white wine into a fondue pot and heat for a few minutes until it simmers.

Add the cheddar, goat, and Emmental cheese, and cook for 20 minutes until well combined. Place the diced red onion and cook over low heat for another 5 minutes; sprinkle with chili powder and black pepper.

Keep the pan warm on a fondue burner, and immerse the pepper strips and chicken strips.

Nutritional values (per serving):

Fat: 22 g - Carbohydrates: 15 g - Protein: 8.6 g - Calories: 290

20) White chocolate and lemon fondue

Preparation time: 20 minutes

Cooking time: 15 minutes

Number of servings: 2

Ingredients:

- 1 lemon peel
- 1 cup white chocolate, chopped into pieces
- 1/2 cup fresh heavy cream
- 2 tablespoons herbal liqueur
- 1 tablespoon lemon juice

Dippers: Sliced apples, Pretzel

Preparation procedure:

Pour the liquid cream, the herb liqueur, and the lemon juice into a fondue pot and simmer for a few minutes.

Add the white chocolate and lemon zest to the pan and cook for about 15 minutes until the mixture is thick and blended. Leave the pot on a fondue burner, and immerse the pretzels and apple slices.

Nutritional values (per serving):

Fat: 15 g - Carbohydrates: 24 g - Protein: 4.5g - Calories: 320

Conclusion

In this cookbook we focus on the characteristics of this ancient culinary skill and provide you with tasty and easy-to-follow recipes that are sure to ignite your passion for dipping tasty treats in cheese, chocolate, and savory variations with oil or broth.

In particular, we emphasized the importance of creativity, simplicity, and sharing in the fondue experience.

This is not just a meal; it is an opportunity to spend time with friends and family around a warm dish of deliciousness. You can dip crusty bread into a pot of simmering cheese, savor juicy meats in broth or hot oil, or indulge in a sweet option like chocolate fondue.

Fondue brings people together and represents unity, friendliness, and fun, crossing cultural boundaries and generational differences.

Fondue reminds us of the beauty of sharing, taking the time to savor each bite, and the sheer pleasure of being together around a table.

Fondue is a refreshing contrast in a fast-paced world where meals are often quick and solitary. It encourages us to slow down, engage in non-superficial conversations, and build lasting memories with our friends and loved ones.

The essence of fondue goes beyond a pot of cheese or chocolate; it reflects the nature and meaning of life itself. In the same way that you carefully select your ingredients and combine them to create an incredible dish, you can act for all other aspects of your life Balance, sharing, and joy are the themes interwoven with the fondue tradition and serve to appreciate life's profound pleasures.

Whether you want to throw a party, celebrate a special occasion, or enjoy an evening with your family, this book will guide you to unforgettable moments around the fondue pot.

Run to embrace the heat and savor the shared joy that fondue brings.

Enjoy!

Made in the USA
Las Vegas, NV
11 December 2023

82472349R00063